# CREWING TO WIN

www.fernhurstbooks.co.uk

# CREWING TO WIN

## Andy Hemmings

*fernhurst* BOOKS

British Library Cataloguing in Publication Data
A catalogue record for this book is available from the British Library

ISBN 1 898660 05 0

Acknowledgements

I would like to thank Paul Brotherton and Ian Pinnell for helming the
various boats. Frank Dunster for patiently driving the photo boat and
Hayling Island Sailing Club for their help.  The Laser Centre kindly
loaned the Laser 5000.


This book, like sailing a crewed dinghy, is a team effort!

Photographs
All photographs by John Woodward except for the following:
Roger Lean-Vercoe - page 16, 27, 75, 89
Peter Bentley - page 23
Christel Clear - page 61
Tim Hore - page 18, 74
Patrick Roach - cover &  page 5


Edited by Peter Milne & Tim Davison
Cover design by Simon Balley
DTP by Alison Cousins
Printed and bound by Ebenezer Baylis & Son Ltd, Worcester

Text set in 10pt Rockwell light

# CONTENTS

# INTRODUCTION

Like so many other people my sailing career started by learning to crew. At that time my father had a small day yacht, and my interest was more in the fishing opportunities that it afforded than in the excitement of sailing. He must have tired of having his boat slowed by the drag of fishing weights, for he insisted I join a small church sailing club and "learn to sail properly".

I was taught to helm and learned quickly, too quickly, for after only a few weeks I felt confident enough to take a boat out on my own, contradicting all club rules. I managed to capsize the boat and end up being rescued, and the result was a six week ban. I never went back to that club and instead, despite not having money to buy a boat, joined the local racing club. Within weeks I began crewing for people on a regular basis and started what has been, to me, both a hobby and a career.

Why crew and not helm? Many things influenced that decision, amongst them money and size, but once I started I began to realise that crewing held as many, if not more, challenges as helming. A good crew is made from experience and dedication, just like a helmsman, but unfortunately is rarely recognised to the same degree. I set out to prove, firstly to myself and then to other people, that a good crew can mean the difference between a successful racing campaign and one that falls by the wayside.

## HOW TO USE THIS BOOK

This book is aimed at both the beginner and the potential champion. The main core is still made up of the traditional crewing skills such as tacking, gybing etc, but to win today you will also need to read the sections on planning, physical and mental fitness, kinetics and so on. While different people have different levels to which they wish to pursue the sport I believe that there is something here of use to everyone.

In Part 1, we look at the things you can do ashore to help you win. Part 2, looks at the 'set pieces' on the water: manoeuvres such as tacking and gybing which you must practice until they are second nature. In Part 3, we discuss the crew's responsibilities during a campaign and during a race, while in Part 4, we give you a clue on how to handle the new breed of twin-wire boats and asymmetrical kites.

I do hope you enjoy reading this book as much as I have enjoyed writing it, and will have a happy and successful career as a crew.

# 1 THE IMPORTANCE OF CREWING

Crewing a boat properly is an art, something that must be worked at and perfected as in any other sport. In tennis, for example, you find very few champions who have not trained, practised and striven.

But you might not want to win the Wimbledon of sailing and this is where our sport is so versatile. Within sailboat racing there is a level of achievement for everyone, from the occasional sailor who aims to have a nice day out, to the Olympic yachtsman whose aim is to win a medal. Everyone can be catered for and, most importantly, everyone has the opportunity to set and achieve personal goals.

Make no mistake, every top crew in the world started at the bottom of the proverbial ladder and had the long, hard, but enjoyable climb towards the top. But where is the top? I maintain there is no pinnacle to this ladder, and this is really why sailing is so appealing. No-one knows everything and to myself and millions of others this is one of the main attractions.

Before I outline the rungs of the ladder, it is worth mentioning the problems that might confront someone thinking of crewing for the first time. Right at the beginning one must consider one's size and weight. Nearly all boats, and especially dinghies, have an optimum crew weight and size. Put simply, the crew must be heavy enough to keep the boat upright in strong winds and light enough so as not to slow the boat down in light winds. So choosing the correct class to sail is influenced by your body dimensions! As an example, a person 5'6" tall and weighing 54kg is not going to

be competitive in a large, powerful boat such as a Flying Dutchman, whereas someone of 6'3" and 95kg is going to look silly sitting in a 420. Much better that they swap boats!

## THE STARTING POINT

The first rung of the ladder is becoming a beginner, and the most traditional means of doing that is to join a local sailing club. Owning a boat is not necessary, in fact it can initially be to your advantage not to, because boats can be relatively expensive to own and maintain. If there are many clubs in your area try to choose one that is both convenient and also active in encouraging new people to get afloat. A quick phone call followed by a visit one weekend will quickly verify the facts.

After joining your club there are two ways of getting out on the water. The first is to put up an advert on the club notice board, stating your interest and contact number. Many clubs have a special crew board for this purpose. Then wait and see if anyone phones. Be honest in your description of both your sailing ability and also the time you have available to sail. Far better to earn your reputation from a helmsman's recommendation than to overstate your ability and subsequently be caught out.

The second is to pack your sailing gear on the day of a race and simply hang around in the hope that some skipper will require your services. (Interestingly, this is the way I started.) There is nearly always someone looking for a crew at the last moment and if you appear keen, willing and able this is infinitely preferable in a helmsman's eyes to having an expert crew who doesn't turn up.

## OPEN MEETINGS

Your period of club sailing will provide you with the groundwork of skill and knowledge to move up to the next rung on the ladder - the open meeting.

Competing at different clubs against different sailors allows new and often more complex tasks to be learned. You will see new boats and different techniques which will often generate new ideas. At an open meeting competition is higher than that experienced at club level, which will give you the incentive to both learn and do better. One point that should not be forgotten here is that open meetings are great fun. There are old friends to meet and new ones to make.

## NATIONAL CHAMPIONSHIPS

The next step is to attend the national championship of your class. In all probability the one name that you will

recognise of all the people that sail your class is that of the class champion. But it is worth remembering that he, like you, once had to go to the class championship for the first time. Do not be put off by the word championship; of course the competition will be strong and you may find the prospect of racing in a big fleet daunting, but the people are the same as at the open meetings and there is just as much fun and learning to be had. For many crews the ladder of achievement stops here; a championship win might well be their ultimate goal and, indeed, if the class is not international there is no next rung up the ladder without a change of boat.

## WORLD OR INTERNATIONAL CHAMPIONSHIPS

Nowadays the world is getting smaller in the sense that foreign travel is becoming much easier. In most international classes the crews looking to progress upwards will eventually find themselves competing abroad and representing their country. The mere fact of having been picked for the team can, by many, be considered achievement enough. But someone has to win and although winning might not seem

an immediate possibility it is at this level where real commitment and dedication can pay off. For non-Olympic classes a world championship win is the top, and make no mistake, to win at this level involves plenty of hard work.

## OLYMPIC SAILING

Numerous people in the past have expressed mixed views about Olympic sailing. To some the thought of campaigning a boat with a view to Olympic selection - and then hopefully an Olympic medal - simply has no appeal. Many others would like to try a campaign but are restricted by time and money. Then there are those that do have a go; these people come away richer in experience regardless of the result. To win an Olympic medal is probably the burning ambition of most crews, but very few ever fulfil that dream and in reality only a slightly larger number ever get picked to represent their country. This final rung on the ladder of crewing is the hardest to achieve and therefore involves the most work and time.

There is a simple saying that I believe sums all this up:

A person who is **100%** committed will often win.

A person who is **50%** committed will sometimes win.

A person who is **5%** committed will never win.

You have to decide what your level of commitment is and plan your crewing career accordingly.

## THE CREW'S SELF-WORTH

Modern day attitudes towards crews are changing. In the past a crew was only on board as ballast and to help handle the sails. Active participation in tactics and decision making was discouraged and so the crew received little or no recognition. The situation has slowly changed, and for a few years now the top helmsmen have realised that to get to the top they need a top crew to sail with. It should also be noted that this applies the other way round: a top crew needs a good helmsman and nowadays many crews can take their pick of drivers.

Today's crew is no longer a second class sailor and he and his helmsman must work together to form a winning team. This was brought home to me recently at a 470 World Championship prize-giving in Brisbane, Australia. The presentation of trophies was preceded by an announcement asking that only helmsmen should come up to collect prizes. A period of stunned silence was quickly followed by boos and catcalls, with every helmsman refusing to go forward when called. The yacht club eventually avoided the potential riot by calling both helmsmen and crew.

While this example isn't exactly earth shattering, it does highlight the increase in stature of crews in the eyes of the yachting world.

# PART ONE

# ON THE SHORE

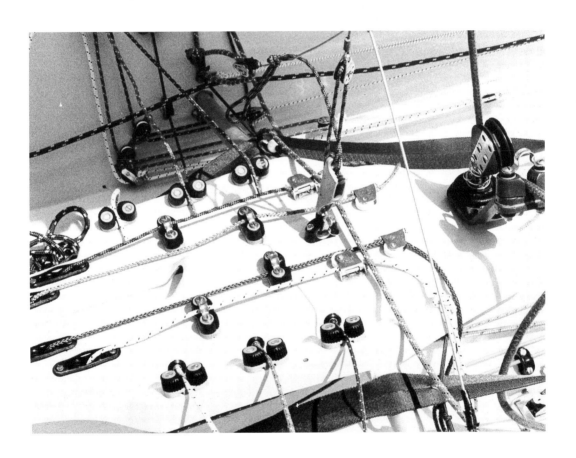

# 2 PLANNING A CAMPAIGN

Whatever level of sailing you decide to aim for, be it a good club racer or to take part in the world championships or, perhaps, the Olympic Games, you will have to do a certain amount of planning. The more important your sailing is to you the more time you will need to spend preparing and planning. I can honestly say that, for my two Olympic campaigns, whenever the sailing had finished for the day the rest of my time was spent either on preparation or planning ahead.

When starting to plan any campaign try to cover the following points.

## GOALS

No, not football type goals, but the level of achievement you wish to attain. Do you have a goal in life? Maybe it's a new house or car, to climb the promotion ladder at work, or perhaps to pass your final and most important exam. Any of these might be very important to you and consciously or subconsciously you have set your goal and your sights on trying to achieve it.

A goal in sailing is no different. Typical sailing goals are to win the class championship; to qualify for the worlds team; to win the worlds! However it is important to realise the difference between setting yourself a realistic target and trying to achieve an impossible dream.

### SETTING YOUR SAILING GOALS

Be honest. How good or bad at sailing do you think you are? Note what you would like to achieve in sailing, bearing in mind your current ability, the time you are able to devote, the cost, etc. We'll use an example here. Let's say you've been sailing your 420 now for two years with moderate success at open meetings, finishing regularly between 6th and 12th overall. A good goal here for your third year would be to finish in the top five at the national championship. This target is not unrealistic for you to achieve, but you will have to work hard to be successful.

Next, set a series of intermediate goals. Picture these as rungs on a ladder, with your main objective perched at the top. These rungs are improvements that you feel you will need to make in order to reach the top.

Division of labour: divide the jobs between you. Here, the helmsman is tuning the rig while I am off getting a weather forecast.

They may be improvements such as better light wind speed, not capsizing on a windy run, achieving consistently better starts, and so on. All of the intermediate goals that you set must be directly within your control. For instance, better light wind speed can be achieved by either practising more in light winds and trying different sail settings or perhaps buying a sail better suited to light conditions. Improvements to your starting can be made by devoting more time to your pre-start checks and routines.

Occasionally your overall goal will need to be altered or modified. If the top of the ladder is proving simply too hard to reach within the time and money allocated, aim for something more achievable - after all you can always shift it back again if the situation changes. It is important to realise that an unattainable target will quickly result in a decreasing amount of enthusiasm.

## MONEY

Unless you are fortunate enough to have a sponsor, the chances are you will be paying for nearly all your sailing out of your own pocket. Sailing can be as expensive, or as cheap, as you wish to make it, but usually a campaign that is well thought out will end up costing less than one badly planned.

Plan the season in advance, working out which open meetings you want to attend, which championships and which training weekends. Travelling and accommodation costs money. If money looks tight in these areas perhaps you should look into double - trailing and sharing a car with a friend. Allow a budget for the maintenance and running repairs of the boat and don't forget to include that of your personal sailing gear. By thinking ahead it is possible to save money on the coming year; for example, many sailmakers offer some discount on new sails purchased during the winter months. Suitable accommodation at the sailing venues should be found and booked early. Often chandlers have an end of season sale which provides an opportunity to replace personal gear at a reduced cost. I am by no means advocating sailing should be done on a shoestring, but a little advance planning can save a lot of money.

## TIME

Some people regard sailing as a pastime, others as an occupation. Only you will know how much time you will be able to devote to the sport. This will influence the type of boat you sail and also the goals you set yourself. For example it would be very difficult to attempt an Olympic campaign with only three weeks' leave per year, as opposed to your competitors who may very well be able to train full time.

For the average person time is often limited. Therefore it is important to use that time as effectively as possible. Part of our 470 campaign included being sent on a time management course; this threw up many ideas which we found useful.

Now plan your racing year. Rank in order of priority the events leading up to the highlights. The priority of each event should be based upon what you hope to achieve from it, and should tie in closely with your intermediate goals. For example, if good starting is something you need to improve, then attending an event which musters only a small entry should not be considered a priority. If time becomes tight, scrub the low priority events first; that way you will still be moving in the right direction towards your long term goal.

Apart from time constraints over the year, time can also be difficult to find on a daily basis. Time to maintain the boat, time to train, time to organise accommodation, etc, all have to be fitted into what is probably an already busy lifestyle. The organisation side of sailing can appear daunting at first, but by sharing the jobs between helmsman and crew, the load can be lessened. Try to complete your share of the jobs in good time and avoid leaving everything until the last moment.

## ABILITY

Two things determine our sailing ability: experience and, to a lesser degree, age. Both have a direct effect upon the class of racing dinghy you will support and the degree of success you can expect. A novice might quickly be out of his depth if placed in a modern International 14. The boat demands a high level of expertise and knowledge, usually gained by an apprenticeship in a less demanding class. Before jumping into a boat assess the level of experience you have, and in most instances don't expect immediate success:

most boats have unusual traits and quirks to be learned first!

## YOUR BUILD

Unfortunately many dinghies are weight sensitive and seem to achieve their best performance with a specific crew weight aboard. Any class and campaign you sail in will have to be directed towards the boat which best suits you. A look around the dinghy park will quickly tell you the size and shape you need to be. But don't forget the main reason why we sail, and that is to have fun. Never let your build be a reason to avoid a particular class that you know is fun, but realise that unless you fit the boat, you will be at a disadvantage when sailing in certain conditions.

## YOUR RESPONSIBILITIES

It is important in any team to have an equal division of labour. If one member is doing more than the others, he can quickly become disillusioned.

Everyone has both strong and weak points, so bear this in mind when various responsibilities are allotted.

In a recent campaign we divided he workload as follows.

I was responsible for:

▲ The major part of boat maintenance
▲ The fitting of any new gear
▲ UK accommodation
▲ Packing the boat prior to travel
▲ Food (on and off the water)
▲ Spare gear for the coach boat
▲ Obtaining the weather forecast

The helmsman was responsible for:

▲ The sails
▲ Foreign travel and accommodation
▲ The car
▲ Currency
▲ Briefings
▲ Handling protests

All the other areas were shared, and while the example used is based on a full time campaign, the principle of dividing the labour applies at all levels.

## THE TEAM

One of the most important contributors to a successful campaign must be effective teamwork. A good working relationship between the helmsman and crew is vital and clashes of personalities should be avoided at all costs. Unfortunately there is still a tendency for those reporting sailing events to concentrate upon the achievements of the helmsman and almost ignore those of the crew. Small wonder so many do not appreciate the importance of really effective teamwork.

Good teamwork is based on a foundation of mutual respect. Both helmsman and crew must respect each other's abilities and work to overcome each other's weaknesses. If one or other loses that regard, a breakdown in the relationship will quickly follow. Nothing slows a boat more effectively than the helmsman and crew being at odds with each other. The successful way to avoid conflict is to adopt a positive attitude. If a mistake is made by either person, forget it and get on with the race. Think positively, tell yourself that everyone is entitled to make a mistake. Learn from it, store it in your mind, and think ahead. An extreme illustration of this springs to mind. A few years ago, I was sailing with a skipper who had an admirable attitude. The regatta had just finished and we were busy packing up the boat. I went to fetch my helmsman's car and began reversing it into a handy parking space. Unfortunately I forgot that the passenger side door was open. Bang! Crunch! Rip. The door hit another car and promptly fell off! Sheepishly I walked up to my skipper and said I had had a little accident and waited for the inevitable barrage of abuse. Instead there was a pause, and then he turned and said "Forget it, it's history now. Any chance we can tie it on?"

His attitude caused a large change in my own and thereafter I began to realise that the winners in life accept mistakes for what they are, and simply get on with the job in hand.

In any team there will always be ups and downs in the relationship: cross words might be said in the heat of the moment or something your partner does annoys you intensely. All of these, if allowed to get out of control, will result in the arguments starting. The easiest way to avoid these is to find out what annoys your sailing partner. The cause of any annoyance becomes obvious after a while: it may be that you are always slow to get changed, or you never fold the sails properly. The answer is simply to identify and try to correct these annoyances, at least in front of your sailing partner! Just like a marriage, a sailing team has to work at the relationship.

# 3 PREPARING THE BOAT & YOURSELF

That famous yachtsman and multiple winner of the America's Cup, Dennis Conner, called his first book *No Excuse to Lose*. His reasoning behind the title and also the way he sailed was that if you cover thoroughly all the aspects that go into yacht racing, you will win. This is never more true than in the things we have direct control over, namely the boat, boat's gear and ourselves!

## BOAT PREPARATION

The boat is a tool. A tool to be used by you, hopefully to win races. Just as a good joiner always works with sharp tools, so your boat should always be properly prepared.

The subject is covered in depth in the Fernhurst books *Sailpower, Tuning Yachts & Small Keelboats* and *Tuning Your Dinghy*.

**The hull** Should be smooth and fair. Scratches and dents must be filled and faired. Keep the hull free from grease by washing regularly with detergent. The type of finish is a personal choice, but I prefer a matt finish produced by rubbing with 400 to 600 grade wet and dry glasspaper used wet. The hull weight should be to the minimum permitted in the class rules and every effort must be made to keep weight out of the ends of the hull.

**The mast and boom** Obviously both need to be strong and free from any permanent bend. Avoid drilling too many holes as breakages will be encouraged in these areas. Wash the spars with fresh water regular and carefully check both the standing and running rigging for signs of wear and tear. If you crew a trapeze boat, pay particular attention to your trapeze wires: a breakage here is both wet and embarrassing!

**The rudder and centreboard** Like the hull - smooth and faired and free from scratches and chips. Protect the edges while not in use with foam and keep them flat and out of the sun when not in the boat or they may warp! The rudder must always be down to minimum weight (avoiding weight in the ends of the boat) while the centreboard is usually nearer maximum weight.

**The layout** Every system on the boat must work; if something does not work well either take it off or change the system. The simpler the boat the easier it is to sail but do have enough fittings on the boat to enable you to alter as much as you need. However, always avoid unnecessary fittings and gimmicks!

**Sheets and halyards** Use low stretch ropes, such as Spectra or Dyneema. These ropes are able to take high loads for minimum stretch and absorb little or no water when wet. Use the smallest diameter of rope commensurate with comfortable handling.

**The sails** Take good care of the sails; they are the engine of the boat. Avoid letting them flog, wash regularly and store dry. Consider a sail programme. We usually replace masts, booms, etc, when they look like breaking, but sails need to be replaced long before that point. Any new sail is only `fast' for a limited period of time. Once that period has been exceeded, the performance of the sail will gradually decrease. Bearing that in mind, you need to introduce sails into the sailing programme giving thought to the age of the sail in relation to your goal for the year. Ideally the sail should be tried and tested before the event, but not for too long or performance will drop. As a guideline, we concluded during our most recent Olympic campaign that whereas a mainsail might be used fairly extensively before it was needed for a main event, the performance of the jib and especially the spinnaker, was subject to much more rapid deterioration. Never use new and untested sails at a big championship.

## PHYSICAL PREPARATION

This is a side of our sport which is gaining in importance. Physical fitness cannot be ignored, especially by crews. How fit you need to be depends on both the level to which you are sailing and on the type of boat. The higher the level, the fitter you should be. To fitness we should probably add agility and suppleness as well. As a rule the trapeze crew must have good all round fitness, but must also be agile, co-ordinated and supple, while the hiking crew needs greater strength especially in the leg and stomach regions.

What exercise you take is up to you, but running, swimming and cycling are the exercises most people identify with, followed by aerobics and gymnasium workouts. There are no short cuts to getting and subsequently staying fit, but

## ympic Games Run up (Full-time)

▲ Monday - AM Run (50 -100 mins)
    PM Swim (30 - 40 mins )

▲ Tuesday - AM Run (20 - 30 mins )
    PM Gymnasium ( light weights )

▲ Wednesday - AM Run (50 -
    100 mins)
    PM Swim (30 - 40 mins)

▲ Thursday - AM Run (20 - 30 mins)
    PM Gymnasium (strength
    exercises )

▲ Friday - AM Run (20 mins)

▲ Saturday - Sailing (no training)

▲ Sunday - Sailing (no training)

## National Championship Run Up (Part-time)

▲ Monday - No training

▲ Tuesday - Run (40-50 mins)

▲ Wednesday - Swim (30 mins)

▲ Thursday - Run (30 mins)

▲ Friday - No training

▲ Saturday - Sailing (no training)

▲ Sunday - Sailing (no training)

whatever form of exercise or fitness training you decide to take, make sure you enjoy it. Without enjoyment your level of commitment will quickly wane.

As an illustration I've used my weekly training routines for both a full time and part time campaign.

On top of this routine, I also do stretching exercises to improve my suppleness, co-ordination and movement around the boat.

As you can see the programme for a national championship is a good deal lighter than that for the Olympics, relying much on the fact that the best fitness training for sailing is sailing!

The bottom line, however, is that while you don't need to be Carl Lewis in order to win dinghy races, your fitness is an integral part of the winning formula. You will hike longer and harder, trapeze better, move with agility, think more clearly and feel better both during and after the race. A much more comprehensive guide to improving your sailing fitness can be found in The Fernhurst book *Mental and Physical Fitness for Sailing.*

# MENTAL PREPARATION

Your boat is perfectly tuned, your body is like a coiled spring, fit and athletic, you have the fastest sails, are able to make the best starts, know the rules inside and out, but what state of mind are you in? The difference between winning and losing a race can often be determined by the way that you feel on the day, and nowadays top level racing often hinges on the amount of mental preparation undertaken.

I have mentioned already the importance of positive thinking after a mistake has been made. This is just a very small part of mental training and easy for you to develop.

Thinking positively can also be very important to you as a person. Until I was about fourteen years of age I thought that people who were succeeding in life were obviously destined to succeed, call it fate if you will. After a while in competitive sailing it began to dawn on me that the harder I worked, and the more I wanted success, the more successful I became. And the key words here are not only WORK, but more importantly WANT. You will always work hard if you want something badly enough, so it is the wanting that is the priority. I wanted to win. I wanted to win every race, regatta, championship that we entered. My outlook now has changed, I now believe that if someone wants something badly enough they will work hard to get it.

The power of positive thought is enormous, it gives each of us the drive and determination that is so necessary to start winning in sailing.

The Fernhurst book *Mental and Physical Fitness for Sailing* covers sports psychology in detail, but there is a chapter that should be briefly mentioned here, namely Mental Rehearsal. I liken this to day-dreaming, but day-dreaming in a controlled way. Watch any star athlete immediately prior to the start of an event. Notice that in between bouts of warm-up exercises, the athlete will often stop and simply stare ahead or close his eyes. Asleep? No. Rehearsing mentally? Yes. He is simply imagining the race ahead, but in a perfect way. The athlete imagines every aspect, the perfect start, the breathing pattern, pulling ahead, feeling comfortable leading the race, making the last surge for the line, the elation of winning. Now when the race starts the athlete simply puts his or her brain into automatic mode with a feeling of *déjà vu,*

I've been here before, and is comfortable during the race. This may be a simplistic illustration of what many sports have taken to a highly refined and complex level, but it serves to illustrate the basis of mental rehearsal.

In sailing we rehearse mentally nearly all the time, unfortunately often in a negative way. The approach to a windy gybe mark is an inopportune moment to start imagining how cold the water will feel if you capsize. Next you start thinking about the last windy gybe when you ended up in the drink; when you put the boat into the gybe, your brain is already resigned to the inevitable and, sure enough, you capsize!

You can improve your chances by running through the situation in your mind, but this time in controlled surroundings on dry land. Any sailing situation, not just the windy gybe, can be rehearsed mentally, be it a tack or gybe, a spinnaker set or drop. Any sailing manoeuvre or skill that you are finding difficult will benefit from this approach.

Start by sitting quietly for a moment, run the manoeuvre through in your mind, trying to imagine everything that you would feel while sailing: the sounds, feel of the boat, etc. Run through the manoeuvre repeatedly until you are entirely happy with the sequence required. If some part is a little hazy, focus in slow motion until you feel happy. Repeat the rehearsal a while later, and again after that, storing it in your mind. Next time the manoeuvre or skill is used when you're out on the water, the actions should be almost automatic.

Why mention this specifically? Because of all the sports psychology exercises that I have done, mental rehearsal has afforded the most dramatic improvement for me.

I use it repeatedly when crewing on new boats with differing systems and also as an aid to controlling stress in areas of the race that would otherwise make me nervous.

I am convinced that mental rehearsal is one of the most effective tools that a crew can possess.

## WHAT IF?

As part of our Olympic training our coach, Rob Andrews, had us think hard about `What If' situations. A " What If " is how we would react to an unusual situation. Both physical and mental reactions would be involved. The idea being that because we had thought about our reactions beforehand, if any imagined situation became reality we would automatically react in the correct manner.

For example - " What If " your trapeze hook broke? Physical action would be to tie the spare piece of 5mm Spectra carried on board through the eyes on the harness and around the ring, then limit tacks to as few as possible. The intention would be to finish the race without drastic loss of places.

" What If " we were disqualified in the first race? Physical action would be to adopt a safe start for the remainder of the series. Mental action would be to forget the disqualification and think ahead only about the remaining races.

" What If's " can cover anything you care to

think about, both on and off the water. They are another form of planning and preparation and of vital importance to both helmsman and crew. As a crew it is vital that you are mentally and physically as strong as your helmsman.

Opposite: the author in action in the Olympics.

Below: note the 'What if'?' line on this trapeze handle in case the lower weld fails.

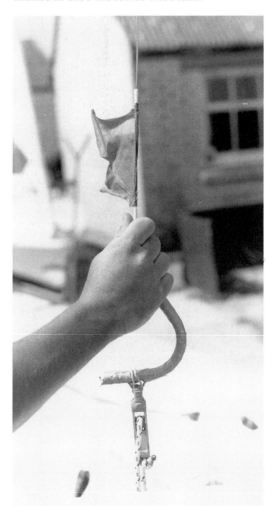

# PART 2

# ON THE WATER

# 4 HIKING

The mere mention of the word hiking (or sitting out) will reduce many crews' leg and stomach muscles to jelly. Unfortunately when the wind is strong enough to facilitate full hiking, there is no escaping the fact that the boat will go faster the harder the crew hikes. While the crew's individual fitness and stamina is a large part of the equation, there are a couple of ideas and items of equipment that will to make the crew's life easier.

## HIKING SHORTS

The main cause of pain in the legs while hiking hard is due to the restriction of blood where the gunwale presses into the back of the thighs. Hiking shorts are padded with

either stiff closed-cell foam or short lengths of batten. This padding spreads localised pressure and helps to reduce the pain and cramps many crews suffer. While many traditional hiking crews regard hiking shorts as unnecessary and possibly a sign of weakness, I maintain that any gear which makes a crew more efficient is worth pursuing.

## BOAT LAYOUT

The boat's layout must be sympathetic with a hiking crew. Every control that needs to be adjusted often when the crew is fully hiked, must be positioned in such a way that he can reach and make the adjustment without coming inboard. Toestrap adjusters, cunningham, spinnaker pole uphaul and downhaul, mast ram, jib fairlead adjusters etc should all be led to a position on or near the boat's side. Use any fittings or ideas allowed to make the effort of hiking easier. On many boats the crew can ease the strain on the legs by keeping hold of the jibsheet and thereby supporting some weight on the arms. To take this a stage further and to avoid accidentally pulling the jib in, crews have fitted a cleat on each gunwale in which the jib sheet can be jammed and hung off on the windward side. Check your class rules carefully to establish that this is permitted.

**Hiking shorts allow the blood to circulate longer to the backs of the legs.**

**The most efficient hiking position to keep the boat flat is with straight legs. If you can't keep your legs straight, bend them for a rest.**

# HIKING TECHNIQUE UPWIND

The most efficient hiking position is undoubtedly sitting out with straight legs. The further out you can sit the more righting moment you are exerting and the flatter and faster the boat will go. However the length of time you can hold this position is limited by your strength and stamina. Unless you are pretty fit, this duration of time will be fairly short. Therefore the effort of straight-leg hiking should be saved for crucial moments in the race, such as the start, a lee bow tack, or a close crossing on port tack.

For the rest of the time you will need to adopt the more comfortable bent-leg hike which makes far less demands on your muscles and causes only a small decrease in the boat's performance. By adjusting the toestrap length and in some boats their lateral siting, a reasonably comfortable position can be found. Remember that in flat water you will need to move slightly further forward and in heavy winds further aft to keep the correct boat trim. As you move forward or back make use of the adjusters to maintain the correct height and comfort of the toestraps.

# HIKING ON A REACH

Once the boat has borne away onto a reach, you must adopt a slightly different hiking position. To begin with the boat will be heeling less and may even incline slightly to windward, so your backside will need to kept clear of the water to avoid drag.

When a gust hits, lean out hard to put as much weight outboard as possible, keeping the boat flat and going fast. In the lulls briefly hike straight-legged in order to raise your body clear of the water. If the lull continues, shorten the straps and sit inboard slightly to prevent the boat heeling too far to windward. Look upwind to anticipate the next gust, and move back outboard again a second or two before the gust hits. The gust will now push the boat upright rather than heeling it over to leeward. This will improve the boat's acceleration.

## TO HIKE OR TRAPEZE

How soon should the crew of a trapeze boat change from hiking to going out on the wire? The answer seems to be earlier than you might think.

In classes such as the 470, Fireball, 505 and 420 the crew, once hooked onto a high trapeze ring, is able to move smoothly and efficiently in order to balance the boat. In light airs many crews start by trapezing and balancing the boat from the centreboard case. The art here is to trapeze very high, so that when a gust heels the boat you push off the centreboard case and swing your feet nimbly onto the gunwale.

Only very occasionally should the crew of a trapeze boat hike instead of hooking on and trapezing, and this seems to be in very choppy conditions with little wind. Sometimes in these conditions the helmsman, playing the waves, finds it necessary to luff hard: if you cannot move far enough inboard and quickly, the boat will heel to windward badly, upsetting the balance and speed of the boat. By hiking in these conditions you can throw your weight inboard to counteract excessive heel and then quickly back outboard again when the rig begins to drive again.

If the boat has no forward toe straps, use the underside of the centreboard capping to hook your feet under.

**Below: the crew's toestraps. On the left the toestraps are loosened for beating, and on the right the toestraps are tightened for reaching: this will keep your backside out of the water.**

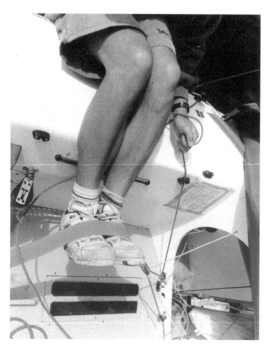
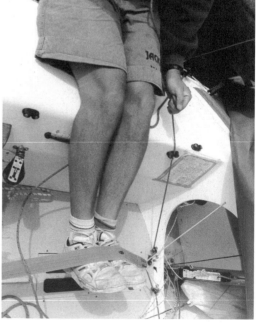

# 5 TRAPEZING

Most modern two-man racing dinghies are trapezed. The trapeze allows an extension of the crew's skills, requiring strength, agility, balance, and sometimes nerve! Let's take a look at some of the specialised equipment involved.

## THE TRAPEZE HARNESS

Just as on a hiking boat, comfort is very important: nobody thinks or acts his best when in pain! There are three distinct types and you should choose the one which you find the most comfortable.

**Note the trapeze harness needs to be tied tightly to your body.**

The standard under-crotch harness is the most widely used and its hook may be held tight to the body with either webbing and buckles or rope and knots. I prefer the rope and knots system as, once tied tight, they rarely slip under load, a problem that can occur with webbing and buckles. The downside of rope is that the harness cannot be removed quickly, either in an emergency or for a quick call of nature! The under-crotch harness does not suit everyone and certainly, if not positioned properly, can cause discomfort. Many new harnesses have done away with the strap under the crotch and replaced it with straps around each leg. These straps free the region of discomfort from load and allow the crew greater freedom of movement. However they do allow the hook to move further away from the body and while the hook can be allowed a couple of inches play, try to have it tied or buckled as close to the body as possible. This means that hooking on and off is positive and avoids the situation where the point of attachment has run out of height adjustment and your backside is still on the gunwale!

Another harness to consider is the nappy type. Made from sailcloth, this harness has no hook rope, buckles, ties etc. Your legs simply slip into the harness which has been made to fit you personally. The advantage of this type is its light weight and simplicity, however the drawbacks are evident if you either put on weight or need to wear extra layers of clothes under it. Both will mean the harness will get very tight and possibly uncomfortable.

A chopped trapeze handle, with simple clamcleat adjuster. The height of the handle is vital.

Boots for sensitive trapezing. They should have soft, rubber soles which wrap around the gunwale for 'feel'.

Other equipment that the trapeze crew needs to consider includes the different types of handles on the market and the height at which to have them. Again, personal choice prevails as to the type, but make sure that the handle is easy to grab and hold, especially when your hands are cold and wet. Avoid plastic handles with plastic load bearing points; these fail after a while resulting in an involuntary swim! Stainless steel welded handles need to have the welds checked periodically. At the first sign of rust in or around the weld, replace them.

The height of the handle is vital. Too low and you cannot trapeze high enough, especially important in light winds. Too high and you will not be able to reach the adjuster when trapezing low in strong winds.

As a guideline sit on the side of the boat facing inboard and the handle should be at eye level. Not only does this eye level height allow full range of adjustment, it also means that the handle will automatically fall into your line of vision during a tack or gybe.

Finally, your personal sailing gear should be considered. The correct footwear can make a large difference to both movements around the boat and also to avoiding slipping on the gunwale. I prefer light-soled wetsuit boots in preference to the popular ankle type. It is important that movements around the boat are light and not clumsy, so avoid thick soled heavy boots. After all, a trapeze crew should move like a ballet dancer and I've yet to see a ballet performed in wellingtons!

## WEIGHT JACKETS

In many classes, both trapeze and hiking, the class rules permit the use of weight jackets. A weight jacket is either a water-holding or water-absorbing jacket, designed to add weight to the person wearing it (normally the crew).

Before we cover this subject briefly it should be noted that medical science is beginning to agree that artificially increasing one's weight in this fashion is not good for the body. Many classes, therefore, have either reduced the permitted weight or banned these jackets. In the next few years I would not be surprised if they are banned from dinghy racing altogether.

However, while individual classes permit the donning of weight jackets people will carry on using them because they do make a significant difference to boatspeed.

The most common jacket is the water-filled type, worn high on the chest.

**The water in a weight jacket should be as high as allowed: around your shoulders is ideal.**

The IRYU outlaws jackets that extend more than 30mm above shoulder height so this type puts the weight as high as possible without infringing the rule. Velcro straps extend around the chest, securing the jacket tightly but allowing it to be removed within 10 seconds, which is also compulsory.

**Going out on a trapeze. Raise the ring slightly, hook on and slide out, pushing first with yout front foot.**

The other type has water-absorbent material sandwiched together. This type of jacket has to be soaked in the water prior to the start and thereafter relies on spray to keep it saturated.

Often the race will start with you wearing weight, and then during the race the wind might die. The water-filled jacket can be emptied to get rid of unwanted extra weight but the fabric type cannot. The most advantageous place to stow the jacket is slung over the side of the centreboard case between the helmsman and crew. This puts the jacket on or near the centre of pitching where it will exert the least detrimental effect while you are racing.

If, just before the start of the race, the decision of whether to wear the weight or not is unclear, go with the greater percentage of the fleet. If most people are wearing weight, so should you.

## BASIC TRAPEZING TECHNIQUES

Today there are more classes than ever granting one or often more crew members the pleasure of trapezing. Modern dinghy classes provide at least one member of the crew with the excitement of trapezing. The newcomer to the trapeze might find the prospect of being suspended by a thin wire above the cold sea whipping by beneath somewhat unnerving but once the basics are mastered and confidence has been gained the fun and thrills begin!

We've looked at the equipment needed to get you out there, so the next step is to learn the three basic actions that are the foundation of good trapezing technique.

## GETTING OUT

Cleat the jib, but keep the sheet near at hand. Raise the height of the trapeze ring to just clear of the deck, so that you are easily able to hook on. Hook on and then pick up the jibsheet in the hand which is closest to the stern of the boat then, with your forward hand, take some of your weight on the handle. Slide outboard and drop your backside over the gunwale, this takes your remaining weight on the harness and puts your centre of gravity out over the side of the boat. Here goes the big step! Bring your forward foot up toward you, until your toes are on the gunwale.

Push out with your forward leg and at the same time slide your back foot also towards the gunwale. Then push out with your back foot, letting the jib sheet run through your hand. Both feet are now on the side: keep them about 12 inches apart until you get used to the boat's movements.

Lean back until the shoulder straps of the harness take the weight of your upper body and let go of the handle.

Bingo! You're out there!

## STAYING PUT

Often the boat will be like a bucking bronco subject to sudden accelerations, decelerations, bumps, bangs, etc, all trying to dislodge you from your perch.

After a while, with more trapezing experience, you will notice that staying put becomes much easier. But for the first few ventures there are a few tips that can be used to make your life easier.

In most boats you will be trapezing a few feet aft from the mast position, so your body will naturally have the feeling of wanting to fall forward, towards the bow.

**To come in lift your back foot and slide in, at the same time bending your front leg.**

Stabilize yourself by pushing slightly with your front leg and at the same time lean back a few inches towards the stern. Hold the jibsheet tightly in your aftermost hand and keep your feet about 6 inches apart so you can anchor yourself to the boat's side.

## COMING IN

First warn the helmsman that you are coming in, so that he can ease the mainsheet to depower the mainsail. Then grab the handle in your forward hand and take some of your weight off the trapeze hook. Lift your back foot and slide it in over the gunwale at the same time bending your front leg. When your backside is touching the gunwale lift yourself over the edge and sit on the tank.

Unhook the ring and ease the jib slightly. You are now ready to tack or gybe if required.

## ADVANCED TRAPEZING TECHNIQUES

Top trapeze crews share the qualities of agility, balance and confidence. All have to be supple, and be able to move with a light nimbleness around the boat. Nothing slows a boat more quickly during a manoeuvre

than the crew crossing the boat like a charging elephant. Many crews, realising the importance of smoothness of movement, include in their training routine either ballet or aerobics.

As a trapeze crew's confidence grows, the ability to move quickly and surely around the boat becomes increasingly important, and very quickly the crew will need to learn the more advanced trapezing techniques.

## USING THE ADJUSTERS

The crew's height above the water is altered using the trapeze adjusters. The aim is to trapeze as low as possible, wind and water conditions allowing. When the boat's rig is at maximum power or you are overpowered get as low as possible; in light winds trapeze higher.

Sometimes the waves do not allow a low trapeze position. Too low and your body will be going through rather than over the waves. This slows the boat and will encourage you to be washed off the side. Raise your adjusters, sacrificing a small amount of righting moment in favour of a dryer, quicker ride.

In gusty conditions your height will need to be adjusted continually and the secret is to anticipate the lulls and gusts and to alter your height just prior to each change of wind speed. By so doing the boat will accelerate faster in the gusts due to your providing more power, while in the lulls the boat will not heel too far to windward and lose speed.

**Adjusters. Here you can see I'm holding the adjuster line, ready to lower or raise my body in the gusts and lulls.**

## WIRE-TO-WIRE TACKING

Unless roll tacking, all boats lose speed when tacking. A trapeze boat is particularly susceptible as the action of the crew coming in, unhooking, tacking, hooking on, going out, etc, all takes time.

The longer the crew stays on the wire before the tack and the quicker he gets on the wire after it, the faster the boat will go. All a wire-to-wire tack does is eliminate the slowest part of the tacking process, namely the unhooking and hooking on before going out. On hearing the call "Ready to tack" you take nearly all your weight off the hook by pulling on the handle. The trapeze shock cord return will pull the ring clear. Your entire weight is now taken on your forward arm; wait until you hear the call " tacking " then uncleat the jib while at the same time sliding inboard.

Cross the boat as quickly as possible picking up the new jib sheet en route and instead of sitting on the gunwale to hook on, grab the handle and go out hanging onto the handle with one hand and taking the jibsheet in the other. When fully out and still hanging onto the handle, sheet the jib fully home and drop the sheet between your legs gripping it between your knees. Now use that free hand to reach for the ring and hook on. Finally, pick up your jibsheet again.

## WIRE-TO-WIRE GYBING

As with tacking, the quicker the crew is able to get onto the trapeze after a reach-to-reach gybe the faster the boat will accelerate. This is especially important at the gybe mark because if you gybe faster than your competitors you may be able to overtake someone who is slower or get into

a position to prevent being overtaken yourself.

Once you've swapped the pole over (see chapter 11) take the spinnaker sheet in one hand, set the sail, then grab the handle with the other and swing out. Hang on the handle while using the hand with the spinnaker sheet to try and push the ring under the hook. Don't panic if you miss first time, you're not that weak! Try again.

## TOP TIPS

Finally, some tips to make life easier on the trapeze.

Use continuous jibsheets; that way the slack in the windward sheet can be taken up before the tack, and you never lose the end.

On the final tack before arriving at the windward mark, raise the ring slightly. After rounding and hoisting the spinnaker

you will find it much easier to hook on and swing out on a slightly higher hook.

When trapezing low in rough water keep the tail of the adjuster rope ready in your hand. But if the top of a wave is about to hit your back but without giving sufficient warning to use the adjuster, try grabbing all parts of the adjuster rope between the ring and the handle and pull sharply towards you. Your back will jerk up a couple of inches, hopefully clearing the wave.

**Wire to wire tacking. When you gain confidence, tacking 'wire to wire' means you unhook and hook on while hanging on the handle.**

# 6 SAILING UPWIND

Understanding how to control sail shape to suit varying conditions is of the utmost importance.

## THE JIB

The jib is designed to increase the speed of the airflow across the mainsail. By constricting and increasing the speed of airflow between the two sails, the air pressure on the leeward side of the main is reduced, thereby causing a significant difference of pressure between the two sides of the sail. It is this difference that partly produces the boat's forward drive.

    The aim when setting up the jib is to induce the greatest pressure difference possible, without stalling the flow. So it is vital that the crew is familiar with the shape of the sail and understands the various effects each control has on it.

**Adjusting the jib tack manually on a 470.**

## JIB HALYARD TENSION

In most classes of dinghy the jib halyard is the primary way of tensioning the rig, with the forestay reduced to the secondary role of insurance in case of halyard breakage. But how tight or loose we have the halyard and consequently the jib luff wire, also affects the shape of the sail, which in turn has a direct influence on the boat's performance.

    If we tension the jib halyard, the distance between the luff and leech of the

**The shape of the sail veiwed as though it's cut in two. We can see where the depth and fullness is located in relation to the width of the sail.**

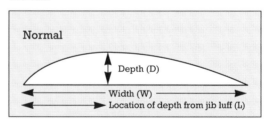

Normal
Depth (D)
Width (W)
Location of depth from jib luff (L)

**Tightening the jib halyard: the depth decreases and moves back.**

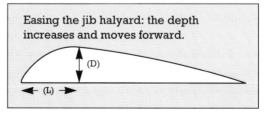

(D)
(L)

**Easing the jib halyard: the depth increases and moves forward.**

(D)
(L)

sail increases, making the depth of the sail decrease and move back. If we reduce the halyard tension the depth increases and moves forward.

## JIB LUFF TENSION

Leaving the halyard tension aside for a moment, we can also alter the position of the depth of the sail, by adjusting the jib tack.

The tension is typically controlled by a simple rope lashing. Pulling down and increasing the tension brings the depth forward, at the same time making the entry (fullness of the jib luff) fuller. Ease the tension and the depth will move back, making the entry flatter. Both of these controls need to be adjusted in conjunction with each other and to suit the conditions prevailing for the race. In light air and especially in choppy water use a fairly low halyard tension.

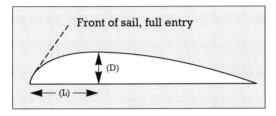

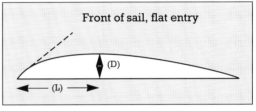

Pull down on the jib tack and the depth moves forward, making the entry full.

Ease up on the jib tack and the entry becomes progressively flatter.

Pull the adjuster tight for heavy airs - note how the camber is pulled forward.

In light air, the tack adjuster is loose, giving a flat entry, with wrinkles at the luff.

Fairlead positions. Above: up and down
adjustment only.
Right: both up and down and inboard and
outboard adjustment.

This means the depth will be forward, so
little luff tension will be used. Both
adjustments add power to the sail, and as
we are not seeking to point very high (the
boat will stall) these settings are ideal for
punching through the waves. If the water is
flatter, the boat is able to point higher so
increase the halyard tension yet keep the
luff tension light.

In strong winds the halyard tension is
higher and the sail therefore flatter. Pull
down on the jib luff to pull the depth
forward, making the entry fuller and the
boat easier to steer. This action also opens
the leech of the sail, de-powering the sail as
is required in windy conditions.

## THE JIB FAIRLEAD POSITION

If we alter the angle at which the jib is
sheeted, we also alter the leech tension. If
we then alter the sheeting position
sideways in the boat, we alter the leech
position in relation to its distance from the
mainsail. These are fundamental controls to
ensure correct setting of the jib.

If we pull the fairlead down, or ease it
forward in a boat with tracks, the tension on
the leech increases. Easing the lead or

moving it back on the track reduces the
tension in the leech. In very light and very
strong winds the leads should be eased up
(or back) to encourage the leech to twist.
A twisted leech is de-powering in strong
winds, but in very light airs encourages the
wind to flow correctly around the sail.
When sailing in light and medium winds
the leads need to be pulled down. This
closes the leech, adding power and
pointing ability, however it is important not
to close the leech too much and
consequently over-choke the air flowing
between the sails. The correct fairlead
setting is indicated in two ways. First, if the
mainsail is set up correctly with respect to
the mast bend, outhaul, etc, and there is
backwinding at the luff of the sail, this is a
good indication that the leech of the jib is
too closed, caused either by the leads
being too far down or too far inboard, or the
jib being sheeted too hard. Ease the sheet
slightly and move the leads up (or back).

Second, look at how the luff telltales

Ease the leads up to twist the leech in very light or strong winds.

Pull the leads down to increase power and pointing ability in medium winds.

are behaving.  If, when sailing closehauled, the bottom set are flowing together yet the top windward telltale is lifting this indicates that the leech is too open: if the top windward telltale is stalling whilst the bottom is lifting the leech is too closed. Again move the leads and perhaps alter the sheet tension to compensate.

Finally, the athwartships or sideways adjustment alters the distance the leech of the jib is away from the luff of the mainsail (the slot).  Too close and the mainsail will backwind (even with a twisted leech), too far away and the airflow is not being squeezed hard enough.  By trial and error or by following the sailmaker's recommendations you will end up with a good all round setting.  From here, if the water is flat, it might be possible to bring the lead inboard slightly and reduce the slot.  If the wind is strong, it nearly always

pays to move the lead outboard, opening the slot and de-powering the boat.

## JIB SHEETING

The final jib control is very much to hand, namely the jibsheet.  How hard the sheet is pulled in when going upwind is dependent on the conditions and also the fairlead position.

If the fairleads are up (or back) the sheet tension will only really affect the shape of the bottom of the sail, and have little influence on the jib leech which will be well twisted.  This combination is ideal for strong winds when the sail should be flat and de-powered.  When the fairleads are further down (or forward), a set-up more suitable for light and medium winds, the jib sheet tension has less effect on the shape at the base of the sail, but more on the tension of the leech. The difference between an open and closed leech is only a matter of altering the sheet tension by a relatively small amount.

It is important that you have a visual mark on the jibsheet that refers to a calibration point on the boat. This way fast settings and tensions can be easily reproduced and with confidence as to their accuracy.

On top of all these settings and tuning, the golden rule - that the jib must be played as much as the mainsail - should not be forgotten. Any gust, lull, overall increase in wind strength, adjustment to the mainsail, etc, means that the jib must be altered as well. If the wind is stable and constant, the occasions you will have to alter the jib might be limited to changes when sailing in sudden patches of choppy water (ease the sheet slightly) or if the helmsman needs to point (sheet slightly harder) or foot (ease sheet slightly). However once the breeze becomes gusty and patchy the time spent altering the jib will increase. When the breeze is very strong play the sheet continually. Ease the sheet in the gusts, allowing the boat to accelerate and stay level. Once the boat is moving or the gust dies sheet the sail back in slightly. Remember the helmsman will being doing the same with the mainsail so it is vital that the actions are co-ordinated so the slot between the sails remains the same.

## UPWIND BOAT BALANCE

Boat trim is the way the boat floats fore and aft in the water. The way the boat floats sideways (or athwartships) is called balance.

**Exert more righting moment by bringing your arms up to head level.**

**In light winds, sit low down and well forward.**

As the crew, you are responsible for a good deal of the boat balance and your aim is to work at keeping the boat flat unless leeward heel is desired (such as in very light airs). If the boat is allowed to heel to leeward many things happen. First, the centreboard loses lift, causing the boat to slip sideways. Second, the helmsman will have to steer more coarsely to maintain his course. This causes increased drag and slows the boat. Third, the sails will have to be over-eased to compensate, thereby losing power and forward drive.
Too much windward heel has similar effects.

The key to keeping the boat balanced is anticipation. By glancing upwind it is possible to read the wind coming down towards you. A gust registers on the water as a darker patch, a lull as a lighter one. Just before a gust hits is when you should make your move to balance the boat. If you leave moving until it actually hits, you will be too late and the boat will heel before you have time to correct. As the gust approaches try to heel the boat slightly to

windward (about 5 degrees). If you're in a hiking boat, apply some extra effort for a few seconds. A trapezing crew should try and achieve the same effect. However, if you are already semi trapezing (trapezing with bent legs) straighten your legs and if necessary lower yourself on the adjuster. If you're trapezing flat out already, now is the time to put one or both arms above your head to shift your centre of gravity as far outboard as possible.

Now, as the gusts hits, the boat will be pushed upright, instead of heeling to leeward.

The opposite applies in lulls. The boat must be kept flat for as long as possible, so there is no benefit in allowing it to heel to

**In stronger winds, move back to help lift the bows clear of the water.**

leeward before the windstrength drops. Instead you must be quick to move your weight inboard as soon as the lull is felt. For the trapeze crew, this means bending your knees and raising your height with the adjuster. For the hiking crew the action is to slide inboard while keeping the boat flat.

# UPWIND BOAT TRIM

Let's look at some general rules regarding boat trim.

**Light winds** The main factor stopping a boat going faster in light winds is wetted surface drag. Wetted surface is the area of hull immersed in the water. The greater that area, the greater the drag. So the first action in light winds is for the crew to move forward two or three feet in the boat. As most dinghies have a flat area aft to provide inherent stability, the action of moving forward is to lift some of that area out of the water and so decrease drag. At the same time, if the wind is very light, heel the boat to leeward slightly. This encourages the sails to fall into their required shape, and also gives the helmsman a slight positive feel on the tiller.

Keep the crew weight in the boat as low as possible. This will probably mean your sitting or squatting on the floor, but by keeping low you are reducing the overall windage and keeping the pitching moment of the boat to a minimum. If possible avoid sitting on the leeward tank or deck. In this position you would obstruct the air flow between the mainsail and jib and increase the overall windage. Much better that you sit low down to leeward inside the boat. Should it need to be heeled slightly have the helmsman slide inboard.

**Medium winds** Once the breeze

increases, the boat will sail at its fastest by maximising the waterline length. As the crew, you will need to hike or trapeze in a position fore and aft that keeps both the transom and the bow just touching the water. In most instances this position will be somewhere opposite the middle of the centreboard case. If the water is choppy, move back just enough to stop the bow digging into the waves and slowing the boat.

Keep the boat flat not only fore and aft, but sideways as well. If the wind is gusty, look upwind and anticipate the variations in strength.

Again, in an effort to reduce pitching make sure that the helmsman is positioned immediately behind you, and not several feet further back.

**Strong winds** Normally, the stronger the wind the larger the waves, so the first action of the crew is to trapeze or hike further aft. This lifts the bow and helps the boat go over, rather than through the waves thereby helping to maintain maximum forward speed and reduce the chance of a capsize caused by the boat slowing and the sails suddenly becoming overpowering. Most trapeze dinghies are able to plane upwind once the wind increases and moving aft encourages the boat to pick up and go slightly earlier.

In order to keep the boat upright and going fast you must provide the maximum righting moment. Trapeze as low as the waves allow, continually adjusting your height as each gust and lull comes and goes. Help the boat accelerate in the gusts by tucking one arm behind your head to get maximum weight outboard. One technique that I use is, as the gust hits drop very sharply using the trapeze adjuster. This flicks the rig momentarily, opens the mainsail leech, and encourages the boat to plane. However, be careful, as done excessively you could be open to a disqualification under rule 54.

# THE CENTREBOARD

Apart from handling the sail controls, another responsibility of the crew is making the necessary adjustments to the position of the centreboard. The position and angle of the centreboard not only affects the amount of leeway (sideways drift) the boat makes, but also how hard or easy the helmsman finds the boat to steer. In light and medium winds the aim is to provide as much lateral resistance as possible so the centreboard is nearly always fully down. Once the boat begins to become overpowered in stronger winds, start to raise the centreboard. This brings the centre of lateral resistance aft towards the centre of effort, making the boat easier to steer around and over waves. Contrary to popular belief, raising the board in such fresh conditions will result in little to no extra leeway, but the boat will be easier to sail and easier to keep flat. A flat boat makes minimum leeway. How much the board should be raised depends on the strength of the breeze. Once the wind is so strong that staying upright is the major consideration, the board must be raised enough to stop the boat tripping in the gusts. This can mean the board is nearly half way up!

In a race at the 470 World Championships in Australia, we had to sail the last beat in about 30-32 knots of wind and very steep large seas. As we came off the top of each wave the boat blew sideways with both main and jib flogging. We found that by raising the centreboard half way the boat stopped tripping over the wave crests and we were able to sheet in

both sails slightly, but most important, the risk of a capsize was much reduced.

Centreboard technology has evolved a long way over the past few years. It is vital you appreciate the difference to boatspeed and feel that can be produced by a small alteration. As with the sails, the centreboard must be worked against accurate reference marks or lines. The most basic system is a number strip down the afteredge of the handle or a series of lines indicating the leading edge angle. Not only is the angle of the leading

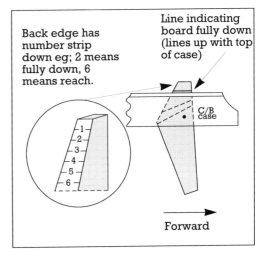

Back edge has number strip down eg; 2 means fully down, 6 means reach.

Line indicating board fully down (lines up with top of case)

C/B case

Forward

edge critical to the feel of the helm, but it also determines the amount of twist acting on the board. If the leading edge is angled forward the tip will twist to windward. Angled aft and the twist will be to leeward. Windward twist is desirable especially in medium winds as it increases the general angle of attack of the board providing greater resistance to leeway. Once overpowered with the leading edge angle raked aft, the leeward twist works well in helping trapeze boats to plane low and fast.

It is my belief that in the majority of classes the biggest speed gains in the future will be made in the field of centreboard design and construction.

# 7 TACKING –
# HIKING & TRAPEZE BOATS

Tacking is most probably the most common boat handling manoeuvre, so it pays to make sure that your technique is good.

Inevitably boatspeed will be lost during every tacking manoeuvre, but it is up to the helmsman and crew to develop a technique which reduces this loss to a minimum. The key to successful, smooth tacks is speed, agility and above all routine. The best crews always have a very set routine, that must be practised until it becomes second nature.

In every condition other than light winds it is important that the boat remains flat going into the tack and flat once the tack is complete. This means staying either hiking or trapezing until the tack begins and

**Roll tacking in light winds fans the air over the sails during the manoeuvre and keeps the boat moving.**

thereafter crossing the boat and quickly resuming your position the other side. If the helmsman and crew are slow, the boat will heel and boatspeed will fall off quickly.

How the boat is laid out and even how you cross from one side to the other, is entirely personal choice. Some crews prefer to have the jib cleats located well forward on the side of the boat and consequently tack facing forwards. Others choose to tack facing aft and therefore have the cleats further back. Whatever your boat's layout, make sure that the system allows the sheet to be cleated or uncleated easily. If the sheet consistently needs two or more upward jerks to uncleat it, the fitting is mounted too high. Likewise if the sheet either slips or keeps uncleating, the cleat is mounted too low.

Experiment with packing beneath the cleats until the best thickness is found.

Also make sure that the bracket on which everything is mounted is the right height. If the bracket is mounted too low, the action of locating the new sheet is made harder because you are stooping to find it. Err towards having it higher rather than lower. That way the new sheet will always be in your line of sight and consequently easier to grab.

Whether to use single ended or continuous jib sheets is again up to you. But I would recommend trapeze crews use continuous sheets. This allows the slack to be pulled from the new sheet while the crew is out on the wire, prior to a tack, and also means that the helmsman can easily adjust the jib when three-sail reaching by leaning forward and picking up any part of the sheet.

## ROLL TACKING

In light winds if a boat is tacked normally it will be at a virtual standstill once the tack is completed.

A good roll tack, however, will mean that the boat is very quickly brought back up to maximum sailing speed.

The tack begins by heeling the boat to leeward slightly. This initiates the turn towards the wind and encourages the helmsman to use less rudder angle - less drag - as he goes into the tack. Next both helmsman and crew move quickly to the windward side, pulling the boat back upright and causing a rapid increase in the windspeed over the sails. The jibsheet is held, backing the jib and spinning the bow through the eye of the wind quickly, then released and the new jibsheet sheeted home. Both crew and helmsman stay heeling the boat until the new heading is reached and the sails are filling. Then according to the wind strength, one or both members of the crew move quickly across to the new windward side, bringing the boat back upright again, causing a fanning effect with the sails.

The basic technique is applicable to both hiking and trapeze boats. Extra roll can be achieved, if needed, by the crew grabbing the trapeze handle and pulling on the rig.

# 8 THE SPINNAKER

Twisting, curling, bouncing, shimmering, flapping: what a complicated sail the spinnaker seems. Unlike the mainsail and jib which have a mast and stays to control the shape, the spinnaker is supported at the two clews and head only. The airflow around the sail can never be described as stable, quite the contrary; with the spinnaker being almost unsupported, the airflow is constantly moving and changing, so in order to achieve the sail's full potential the crew has to be skilled when handling it. Skilled in both the understanding of the fundamentals of spinnaker trim, and also in the art of concentration. The sail demands constant attention and adjustment and if trimmed correctly will help you gain many yards over the opposition. Trimmed incorrectly the spinnaker becomes a very efficient air brake!

Let's start by looking at the controls and equipment used.

## THE SPINNAKER GEAR

### THE SHEET AND GUY

As with the other ropes on the boat, the spinnaker sheets should be of the lowest stretch rope available. When a gust hits, it is essential that the power generated increases the boat's speed rather than being absorbed in the stretch of the sheet and guy. The sail material stretches enough as it is.

Make sure that the diameter of the sheet and guy is as small as feasible. A small diameter rope absorbs little water, is

light and runs freely. However, small rope can be hard on your hands so gloves are important. Where it is handled most often, such as the middle of the spinnaker sheet or the guy just behind the twinning lines, the rope can be tapered up to a thicker size to make handling easier. There are also machine-tapered sheets available on the market which serve the same purpose.

While every effort is made to reduce friction, in windy conditions friction in the form of a ratchet block can make playing the sheet easier and more efficient. These have been developed to make your life easier and I for one always use them. I've seen so many races lost because the crew's arms are tired and the spinnaker consequently overtrimmed.

On a final note, reduce the amount of rope lying around in the boat by keeping your spinnaker sheets (and for that matter all other sheets) to the minimum length.

## THE POLE

The pole is very personal to the crew. I know one brilliant foredeck hand who brings his own spinnaker pole to each boat he sails on. He gets off the aeroplane, sailing gear bag in one hand and 8ft spinnaker pole in the other! While this example is slightly extreme, most top crews personalise their spinnaker poles in some way. The criteria for a good pole and stowage system are:

1. The pole must be as stiff yet as light as possible. Stiff to prevent the pole bending and absorbing power from a gust

and light to make for easy handling.

2. The stowage system must be easy to use and fool-proof. Choose a system within the class rules that is simple. Remember, complicated systems often go wrong when the racing is tight and the wind is strong.

## TYPE OF SPINNAKER STOWAGE

Normally the class of boat will determine whether the spinnaker stowage is either a chute or bags. Both have advantages and disadvantages and if your class has the option of one or the other these must be considered, along with your personal choice of course!

The chute allows quicker hoists and later drops because both the helmsman and crew are sharing the jobs during the manoeuvre, ie the helmsman drops the spinnaker, while at the same time the crew is stowing the pole. It also allows the crew to stay on the wire during the drop, with the pole being stowed when an opportunity arises.

**Solid rope downhaul. This type of downhaul prevents spinnaker pole bounce. When the pole is at the correct height, the crew adjusts the downhaul to lock it solidly. When the pole is removed, the elastitic take up tidies the downhaul away.**

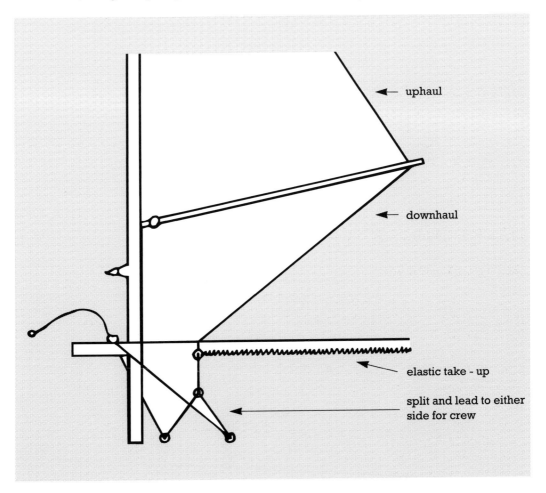

uphaul

downhaul

elastic take - up

split and lead to either side for crew

This is particulary useful on a windy, tight reach dowse. The chute's drawback is the weight of a wet spinnaker up forward. This, according to the spinnaker size, can be as much as 7-14lbs and is located in a far from ideal place, only serving to aggravate the boat's pitching.

The bag system does mean more work for the crew. Some hoists and all drops involve the crew coming inboard to handle

**A leeward hoist from bags. First, raise the centreboard, ease the jib, pick up the pole and take in the slack on the twinning line. Clip the guy into the pole end, put the uphaul/downhaul hook on, push the pole out and pull the twinning line down. The helmsman starts to hoist as soon as the pole is clipped to the guy.**

the sail manually, which in turn means that the manoeuvre takes more time than that involved with the chute. However this disadvantage is outweighed by having the weight of the wet sail in a more advantageous position, which is normally just aft of the mast.

If there is doubt over which option to choose, consider carefully the wind, wave and course conditions that you most commonly sail in.

## THE SPINNAKER POLE UPHAUL AND DOWNHAUL

Often overlooked in importance, yet vital for the crew to retain control over the sail. Again, use low stretch rope to prevent

losing power. Make sure that the downhaul does not allow the spinnaker pole to bounce or move as this only adds to the spinnaker's instability, making it harder to trim. If possible use a solid rope downhaul to lock the pole into place once set, and lead both the uphaul and downhaul tails back to a position both helmsman and crew can reach.

## TWINNING LINES

More and more classes are turning to twinning lines to control the spinnaker guy in preference to the traditional camcleat and hook. They allow the guy to be preset before or during a gybe or hoist. The diagram shows the most common layout,

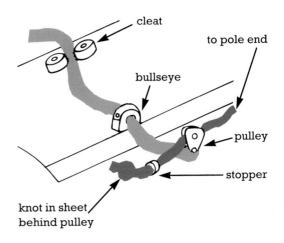

Simple twinning layout.
The knot in the sheet is the correct length for the pole to be 2 - 3 inches off the forestay.

For a windward hoist, throw the spinnaker forward so that it clears the jib, tug the guy to clear any wraps, then connect up the pole. Once the spinnaker is hoisted, note that the helmsman is controlling both sheet and guy.

using a bobble as the stop, but there are many variations of layout that can be used. On windy downwind runs the leeward twinning line can also be utilised to stop the boat rolling. By pulling down on the leeward line, the spinnaker stops oscillating (rolling) from side to side, stabilizing the boat. But normally, of course, the leeward twinning line is loose.

## HOISTING THE SPINNAKER

A good, quick spinnaker set is always important. Watch two boats round the top mark together ready for the reaching leg. If one hoists and sets the spinnaker more

quickly than the other, that boat immediately pulls quickly away, while the other is left looking at a disappearing transom. A good set is a sure way to gain distance or places.

## HOISTING FROM THE LEEWARD BAG

Before the boat reaches the weather mark, make sure everything is ready for the hoist. The leeward twinning line must be uncleated, the halyard unclipped and a glance to see which side the pole is stowed will save a second's fumbling. As the boat bears away ease the jib to trim it for a reach and cleat it. Next raise the centreboard (if not already done by the helmsman prior to or during the rounding manoeuvre) to the reaching or running setting. Grab the pole and put the guy into the piston end, then connect the pole uphaul and downhaul (if not permanently attached). While the

helmsman hoists the spinnaker, push the pole forward (not sideways), clipping the end onto the mast eye. Turn and pull the twinning line hard down, then pick up the sheet from the helmsman who has set the sail. Watch that the helmsman does not sheet and set the sail too early, otherwise putting the pole on and pulling the twinning line down will be very hard. Make sure there is co-ordination between you. If the leg is a reach, either move smartly to prepare to hike or hook on and prepare to trapeze. If the leg is a broad reach or run sit on the gunwale, with one hand playing the sheet and the other the guy.

There will be small variations according to the boat's layout, but the secret to fast hoists is for you to find a routine and then stick to it. As a guide, the time from the boat rounding the mark to the spinnaker set and drawing and crew trapezing or hiking should be no longer than eight seconds!

You will need plenty of practice to achieve this time.

## HOISTING FROM THE WINDWARD BAG

Knowing the course and conditions, there is little excuse for the hoist at the first windward mark being made from anything other than the leeward bag. Thereafter, however, a hoist or two may have to be carried out from the windward side.

As for a leeward hoist, start your preparations well before reaching the mark. Remind the helmsman that it is a windward hoist. Uncleat the halyard and make sure the new windward twinning line is down and cleated and the old one released. If the old sheet (now the new guy) was cleated in a tidy cleat make sure this is uncleated, otherwise the spinnaker will not clear the forestay. At the mark, ease the jib and raise the centreboard (if not already done). Regardless of whether the next course is broad or tight the helmsman will have to bear away onto a broad reach. This ensures that when the spinnaker is thrown forward it is blown clear of the jib luff. If the helmsman holds too high a course initially, the spinnaker will not reach the front of the jib and be blown back between the mainsail and jib. Nothing stops a boat more quickly than a spinnaker set in the slot and pulling the boat backwards! Once the boat has been turned well downwind, move inboard and grab the spinnaker as though it was a rugby ball and pull it up out of the bag. Shout back to the helmsman "Ready?" He should be ready with the spinnaker halyard in hand. On your command "Hoist" throw the sail forward in a similar style to passing a rugby ball, making sure it clears the jib luff. The helmsman will haul on the spinnaker halyard at the same time.

Your next immediate action is to grab the spinnaker guy and give it a sharp tug, clearing the sail of any warps. Still holding onto the guy with your outboard hand reach to the pole with your other hand and clip the guy into the end fitting. Connect the uphaul and downhaul (if not permanent) and clip the pole onto the mast. Finally, pick up the sheet from the helmsman.

If the course is a tight reach the helmsman will have been steering progressively tighter once the spinnaker is hoisted, so your weight will be needed quickly to balance the boat. If the course is a broad reach or run sit down with the sheet in one hand and the guy in the other.

Once again the whole operation should not take longer than eight to ten seconds.

## HOISTING FROM A CHUTE

Because the spinnaker chute is located at the very front of the boat there is no windward or leeward hoist to consider and

**Hoisting from the chute is more straightforward than hoisting from bags. On the approach to the mark, note the helmsman checking that both guy and sheet are ready.**

the sequence of operations is always the same.

Start preparing prior to the windward mark. Pull down and cleat the windward twinning line and make sure the leeward one is uncleated (the helmsman can do the preparation if you are out on the trapeze). At the windward mark ease the jibsheet and raise the centreboard to the reach or run setting. Now pick up the pole and clip the guy into the piston end. Attach the uphaul and downhaul (if not permanently attached) and push the pole forward (not sideways) clipping the other end onto the mast eye. Once the helmsman knows that the pole is connected to the mast he can grab the sheet and sheet in. Move back and pick up the sheet from the helmsman. Prepare to trapeze or hike if the leg is a reach. If the course is a broad reach or run sit down with the sheet in one hand and the guy in the other.

## VARIATIONS ON SPINNAKER HOISTS

There will always be slight variations according to differing layouts and personal preferences. One major variation however is for the helmsman to put the pole on prior to a set. This action saves vital seconds which may help you gain several boat lengths over your competitors. Unfortunately the manoeuvre is restricted to trapeze boats in trapezing conditions and to a leeward hoist for boats with bags. It is advisable to attempt this manoeuvre only when the traffic at the weather mark is pretty light. Note that the tiller must be fitted with a telescopic extension.

The boat is approaching the windward mark on the layline. With about ten lengths to go the helmsman either cleats the mainsheet or hands it to the crew. This decision will be made depending on the gustiness of the conditions. Next the tiller is extended and handed to the crew who now concentrates on steering fast.

The helmsman can speed things up by pre-setting the pole while leaving the crew to drive the boat. In this sequence the helmsman has left the pole hanging, leaving the crew to finish the set.

The helmsman stands up, moves forward and prepares for the hoist in the usual way by uncleating the leeward twinning line and unclipping the halyard.

Because the aim is to preset the pole, the windward twinning line cannot usually be pulled on otherwise the spinnaker will be pulled out of the bag (or chute) too early. With the crew still steering, the helmsman connects the guy and then the uphaul and downhaul and finally clips the pole onto the mast. He moves back and the crew hands him the tiller and the mainsheet.

The boat should now be at the mark. As the boat bears away the spinnaker is hoisted. All the crew needs to do is ease the jib and raise the centreboard and quickly pull the windward twinning line down hard as the spinnaker goes up.

Grabbing the sheet, the crew can then go immediately out on the trapeze. By this means the total time from rounding the windward mark to the set is reduced to about four or five seconds.

In light winds the pole can be preset, but this time by the crew. All the usual pre-rounding checks and preparations are made, with the pole being fully preset. Ensure that the windward twinning line is not pulled on. Alternatively you may choose to leave the pole hanging by the mast, connected to the guy and uphaul and downhaul only. This means the twinning line can be pulled on part or all the way. At the hoist the pole is clipped on to the mast.

I prefer the latter option, because in light winds the action of pulling down on the windward twinning line brings the pole too far aft.

## DROPPING THE SPINNAKER

While a quick spinnaker hoist is obviously

important, it is just as important that the subsequent drop should be as smooth and speedy as possible. It is normal to drop the sail slightly early and concentrate on a good clean rounding, but occasionally it will be necessary to perform a late drop, such as when you want to break an overlap, gain a late overlap, or even just get round the mark in light winds and in a foul tide.

## DROPPING INTO SPINNAKER BAGS

The windward bag is always used for a drop, since in anything but the lightest of breezes pulling the spinnaker in under the jib and into the leeward bag is almost impossible. As you move inboard to reach the pole, hand the spinnaker sheet to the helmsman to keep the sail setting (unless the reach is very tight or windy). Unclip the pole from the mast, uphaul and downhaul and guy and stow it, or hand it back for the helmsman to stow. Grab the guy and shout "Go " as a signal for the spinnaker halyard

to be released. Within the next couple of seconds you must pull the clew and half of the foot towards the bag. The rest of the sail is pulled down hand over hand with as much haste as possible. Finish the packing by stuffing the remaining clew in on top. This means that on the next set, the pre setting of the pole will not pull all of the sail from the bag, just the required clew.

Either the helmsman or you should pull the centreboard down. If it's your job, simply push the head of the board back and down with your inboard leg as you finish tidying the halyard and sheets. Pick up the jibsheet and trim the sail as you round the mark.

## DROPPING INTO A SPINNAKER CHUTE

The spinnaker chute allows the drop to be left until fairly late, and in many instances the helmsman can commence dropping the sail while you are still hiking or trapezing and balancing the boat. To avoid the sheet

accidentally falling over the bow and
subsequently being swept under the boat,
maintain tension on it while the spinnaker is
being pulled in; not enough to make it a
struggle to retrieve, but let the sheet run
slowly through your hand in a controlled
manner. Once the sail is halfway in the
chute, you can remove the pole and stow it.
You can push the centreboard down with
your foot while removing the pole. Tidy the
sheets and pick up the jibsheet ready to
trim as you round the mark.

**When dropping the spinnaker, the helmsman
keeps the sail drawing while the pole is
stowed. Next the halyard is released and the
clew and half the foot are stuffed into the bag.
Notice how, at the end of the drop, the crew is
able to push the centreboard down with his
foot.**

## A BAD DROP

If things start going wrong, a knot in the
halyard perhaps, or a sheet over the bow,
and time is rapidly running out, your first
priority is to get the boat around the mark
and keep sailing. Once the boat is being
driven to windward the problem must be
sorted. If you are out on the trapeze it is
best to stay there and, having taken the
mainsheet and tiller from the helmsman, let
him straighten things out. Either way, the
important thing is to sail as fast and
efficiently as possible until the mistake is
corrected. Remember, if there is another
boat close astern as you go around the
mark, he will have to do two tacks and a few
minutes sailing to pass you, by which time
you should be sorted. If, however, you
panic before the mark and end up missing
it, he will be ahead immediately.

# 9 REACHING WITH A SPINNAKER

Reaching, the really fun part of sailing, is both exhilarating and challenging. Any increase in boatspeed from one boat relative to another will instantly become apparent. Poor technique or bad sail trim is nearly always the cause of poor boatspeed so this leg of the course demands as much concentration and skill as any other.

Before we look at the techniques for reaching, let's review the basic controls that are available to alter the shape and characteristics of the spinnaker.

## THE SPINNAKER POLE HEIGHT

How high or low you fly the pole is determined by wind strength and the angle of the wind to the sail, (ie tight reach, broad reach, run). If the wind is light the sail will be reluctant to fill if the pole is too high. By lowering the outboard end the sail will become more stable and set more easily. Once the breeze increases the sail will need no encouragement to fill, but now the priority is to produce the correct shape.

The spinnaker pole is too high and the head of the sail has become unstable.

The pole is at the correct height, so the luff can curl evenly.

With the pole set too low the leech is very open.

Raising the pole causes the sail to spread the maximum projected area that has been built into it. If the pole is raised too high, however, the sail will become unsupported and unstable.

The best indicator of whether the pole height is correct is the position of the curl in the luff of the spinnaker. If, when the sheet is eased, the sail curls first in the upper half, this indicates that the pole is too low. If the curl occurs first in the lower half then the pole is probably too high. An even curl means the pole is set about right. I must add that this rule of thumb is very general. Spinnakers vary in shape and size according to the class of boat. Only time spent racing and sailing will tell.

Raising or lowering the pole has a marked effect on the leech of the sail.

A low pole will tend to pull the shape of the sail forward. As in the case of a jib or mainsail this produces an open leech.

A pole that is too high will flatten the luff, but increase the depth of the sail further back and close the leech. You must remember that an alteration of pole height affects not only the shape and ease of setting, but also the character of the leech of the sail.

## THE SPINNAKER SHEET LEAD POSITION

Some class rules fix the spinnaker lead positions while others allow the option of

**Too much twist in the leech of the jib causes the sail to set inefficiently.**

**Here the crew is pulling down on the clew to take the twist out of the sail.**

moving the angle the sheet makes with the spinnaker clew. This angle works on a similar principle to that of the jibsheet leads. If the leads are brought forward the effect is to close the leech. Move the leads aft and the leech will open.

## REACHING WITH THE SPINNAKER

Once around the top mark with the spinnaker set, you should run through a mental checklist. First, check that the spinnaker is fully hoisted; if not ask the helmsman to pull in the last bit. Second, see if the spinnaker pole height is correct for the wind conditions and that the angle of the pole is 90 degrees to the apparent wind (look at the burgee if in doubt). If the reach is tight make sure that the forward pole end is held off the jib luff by about two to three inches. This stops the pole bending or even breaking where it touches the jib luff wire. Keeping the pole end away from the jib luff also encourages the pull of the spinnaker forward rather than sideways.

Settle down as soon as possible after the set and concentrate on getting the maximum drive from the sail. Continually ease the sheet until the luff starts curling, then sheet back in slightly, then ease again and so on. If the wind is strong and gusty the sheet must be eased as the gust hits. This ease compensates for the apparent wind shifting aft, and also vents the sail so the helmsman is able to bear away easily. As the boatspeed increases the sail will need to be sheeted back in again. If the boat is planing up and down waves, the acceleration will require the sail to be sheeted harder and any deceleration should be accompanied by a well judged easing of the sheet. A very tight reach where it is a struggle to lay the mark can be made easier by dropping the pole down and tightening the pole downhaul. This opens the leech of the spinnaker, depowering the sail and making it easier to sail closer to the wind.

## REACHING IN A NON-SPINNAKER BOAT

Without a spinnaker the differences in speed between boats will be even smaller so on no account can the non-spinnaker crew afford to relax on the reach. The mainsail and jib must be played continually to get the maximum drive from the rig.

### SETTING THE JIB LEADS

If the jib is eased out onto a reach without altering the sheet lead position, the top of the leech will be much too open. The telltales will indicate that there is far too much twist in the sail from foot to head with the bottom set flowing and the top set breaking. In order to provide maximum drive in boats with adjustable sheet leads it will be necessary to close the leech by moving the leads forward. This not only closes the upper leech, but also makes the base of the sail fuller which is important in producing more power. If your boat has the added facility of pulling the leads outboard (towards the gunwale) as well as forward, this adjustment should be used as well. This outboard movement means that the distance between the mainsail and the jib remains the same as when sailing upwind, whereas if the leads only move forward, with the mainsail eased for the reach, this distance decreases and the slot becomes choked.

If your boat has no lead adjustment then you, or more precisely your arm, can achieve a similar effect. In light and

medium winds, providing you are not needed to balance the boat, hold the jibsheet forward and outboard while sheeting the sail correctly. In heavy winds you will have to forget this method and concentrate on keeping the boat upright.

## TRIMMING THE JIB

Set the leads forward, and if possible outboard. The luff telltales are a useful indicator of whether you have the correct leech tension. Aim to have all the windward telltales luffing together. If the topmost one luffs long before the others, this indicates you should move the lead further forward.

If the mainsail is being constantly adjusted to changes in course angle and differing windstrengths, then the trimming of the jib must follow suit. For instance, as a gust hits, the helmsman will start to bear away and the apparent wind will

momentarily shift aft. Both actions mean you will need to ease the jibsheet quickly. As the gust dies, anticipate the boat coming slightly closer to the wind and the apparent wind shifting forward. Now the jib will need to be trimmed in slightly.

## BOAT TRIM ON A REACH

Where you sit, hike or trapeze while reaching affects both the balance and trim of the boat and, ultimately, your speed.

**Light airs** As with upwind sailing in light airs, one of the main concerns is to reduce the amount of drag the hull is producing going through the water. This drag can be reduced by having both the helmsman and crew sit further forward than usual, thereby lifting the flat stern sections and reducing the wetted area. If the wind is very light heel the boat to leeward slightly; this helps the spinnaker to set. In a boat carrying a spinnaker it is important that the crew maintains a clear view of the sail so the helmsman must be prepared to steer while sitting to leeward and balancing the crew on the weather side. If the boat needs still more heel, the crew must slide inboard as much as required. In a non-spinnaker boat, the crew will need to be to leeward in order to have a good view of both the jib leech and luff telltales.

The centreboard position varies according to how close the reach is: the closer to the wind, the more board will need to be down. However, because the area of the board contributes significantly to the overall drag, the rule is to have as little down as possible until the boat starts to slip sideways.

**Medium airs** Until the boat starts to plane or surf, the helmsman and crew will normally be positioned somewhere in the region of the mid length of the boat. The boat must be kept flat and powered up with the centreboard raised as high as possible and making little leeway.

**Heavy winds** Once the boat is almost continually planing the helmsman and crew should move back. This shift of weight raises the bow out of the water and helps the boat plane more quickly on the flat after-sections. It also stops the bow from digging into large waves and stopping the boat. Maximum speed is gained by keeping the boat as flat as possible, with the centreboard up as much as possible. The faster the boat goes, the less centreboard you will need down. This also lets the helmsman bear away quickly in the gusts without the boat stalling and tripping over the board.

## CREW KINETICS ON A REACH

While some in the sailing world frown upon crew kinetics, no crew nowadays can afford to ignore the speed benefits that can be gained. What are kinetics? They are simply pumping and specific crew movements intended to produce bursts of improved boatspeed. Both the IYRU sailing rules and, possibly, those governing your class control the extent to which you may use physical effort. Make full use of what is permitted in the rules but be sure not to step outside them.

In most classes the wording is such as to prevent pumping of any sail until, on a free leg of the course, planing or surfing is possible. This virtually eliminates pumping in light conditions, but once the breeze increases enough or the waves become large enough, correct and legal pumping can produce significant advantages. You are legally allowed to pump sooner when waves exist than in flat water when only gusts are available to make the boat plane. There can be a significant difference between what is legal on the sea and what is legal on inland water.

As well as pumping, careful decisive body movements are allowed to assist steering and need to be incorporated. We all know that a rudderless dinghy will bear away when heeled to windward and head up when heeled to leeward. Bear this in mind when going downwind, especially in waves. Correct use of body weight to modify lateral trim will help a good deal towards enabling the helmsman to make less use of the rudder to maintain his course.

For example, if you are sailing on a broad reach with spinnaker set, sit on the windward gunwale holding the spinnaker sheet in one hand and the guy in the other. Divide your attention between keeping a close eye on the trim of the spinnaker, while observing the waves around your boat. As the boat catches up with, or is caught up by, a wave, lean in slightly to head the boat up a little and increase the speed. As the wave begins to pass under the boat, make the boat bear away by leaning out. At the same time give the sheet and the guy a smooth pump. Keep the pole squared back as the boat begins to accelerate down the wave, then begin easing it forward once the apparent wind increases and moves towards the bow. As the boat begins to decelerate at the end of each wave lean

**Try to steer the boat by using body weight. Here, the crew is able to make the boat bear away down a wave by straightening his legs. If he bends his legs the boat will head up.**

your body back in to help the boat head up once more to maintain speed for as long as possible.

The same actions can be repeated by trapeze crews, hooked onto a high ring, simply transferring their weight from centreboard case to gunwale and back again.

If the reach is tight and windy, you won't be able to pump the guy. Instead, as the boat reaches the top of the wave, simply jerk the sheet hard and at the same time take a step forward. Once the boat starts to accelerate down the wave face, move sharply back to prevent the bow digging in and stopping the boat. The quick transfer of weight aft will also help to kick the boat forward.

# 10 RUNNING

In the halcyon days of sail, when racing yachts were 100 feet long, sailed by a crew of thirty, and setting not just a few hundred square feet of sail, but thousands, the run was perceived as a time to exhibit the entire sail wardrobe. Every square inch that could be hoisted was hung out on the principle that the more aloft, the faster the boat would go. Rigs falling down, deaths, even boats just being driven under were commonplace because few owners or skippers fully appreciated the limitations of displacement hull speed or the tremendous loads generated in huge rigs.

**When running, the crew must be in a position to sight the spinnaker clearly and control the sheet and guy at the same time.**

Today, our views on running downwind have changed. Few, if any, dinghies put more sail area aloft than necessary when reaching and the game of sailing downwind has become as tactical as going upwind with every emphasis on technique and concentration. Today's crew cannot afford to relax for one second on a run.

## RUNNING WITH A SPINNAKER

As soon as the spinnaker is set you must be in a position to see the luff of the sail clearly. This typically means the helmsman sitting to leeward, with you sitting opposite him and up to weather. In one hand should be the spinnaker sheet and in the other the spinnaker guy.

**In boats that do not carry a spinnaker, the jib must be goosewinged when running.**

This allows the pole to be moved easily forward and back, whilst at the same time keeping the luff of the sail curling with correct sheet tension.

### CORRECT SPINNAKER POLE HEIGHT

The guidelines here are the same as for reaching. Aim to keep the luff curling evenly over its length by lowering the pole if the bottom of the sail curls inwards first; raise it if the top is breaking. If the wind is steady and of medium strength set the pole slightly higher than this, allowing the shoulders of the sail to spread. This will make the sail harder to trim, however, and quicker to collapse. Keeping the sail trimmed correctly demands a high degree of concentration. In light winds and/or choppy water, lower the pole to help support the sail and make it easier to set. If the wind is very strong and simply surviving the run is the priority, lowering the pole will make the sail stable and stop the boat rolling. The leeward twinning line can also be pulled down hard to stop the spinnaker oscillating and the boat rolling.

### THE CENTREBOARD

In light or medium airs you need very little centreboard down. Leave the tip of the board projecting from the case to act as a skeg and provide a small amount of feel to the rudder. A little more board will be needed once the breeze increases to prevent the boat from rolling. In very windy conditions the centreboard might be as much as half down.

**In strong winds, move your weight back in the boat to prevent the bow burying.**

# GOOSEWINGING THE JIB

If the class of boat you sail has no spinnaker the jib will have to be goosewinged on the run. This means holding or, in most cases, poling out the jib on the opposite side to the mainsail. The jibsheet is then used to trim the sail so that it maintains an angle of about 90 degrees to the apparent wind. The act of goosewinging exposes the maximum sail area to the wind and helps to keep the boat balanced. The crew must be quick to set the pole as time spent without the sail fully spread results in lost distance and places.

# BOAT TRIM ON THE RUN

Again, let's subdivide this section into three sailing wind strengths, light, medium and heavy.

In light winds the trim is the same as for

With a wave under the bow, the crew slides forward and both spinnaker sheet and guy are pumped.

As the boat accelerates, the crew slides his weight aft and the boat is heeled to windward to ease the steering.

On decelerating, the boat is allowed to heel a little to leeward so that the helmsman retains feel.

going upwind. Both crew and helmsman should be sitting forward in the boat, to lift the stern and reduce drag. It also helps to set the spinnaker if the boat is heeled slightly to windward. This windward heel means the spinnaker will effectively want to fall into its flying shape and, when used in conjunction with the correct pole height, will make setting the sail very much easier. In order to stop the main boom from wanting to swing inboard the helmsman will need to hold it out physically against the shrouds.

In medium winds which are still not strong enough to allow it to plane, the boat should be trimmed to sail on maximum waterline length with both helmsman and crew sitting approximately mid way fore and aft. Instead of heeling the boat to windward, it should be kept flat.

As the wind rises a little more the boat will be occasionally planing and surfing.

Once this strength is reached the crew and helmsman must constantly adjust the fore and aft trim: moving aft in the boat as it begins to surf and forward again as it slows.

In strong winds, both the helmsman and crew will be positioned two or three feet further back in the boat. By keeping the stern trimmed down, the bows are prevented from submerging into the waves and the boat planes easily on the flat sections at the stern. It is essential that the boat is kept as upright as possible. Any heel to leeward will encourage a broach while a heel to windward will cause the boat to bear off sharply. Both tendencies are likely to result in a capsize.

## CREW KINETICS ON THE RUN

In the old days when dinghy racing was not so competitive the run was often viewed as a leg of the course on which the crew could rest and enjoy the ride downhill. You will not be surprised to learn that those days have long gone. The work rate on the run is as high as any other, and once the wind is strong enough crew kinetics will separate the fast boats from the slow!

Once surfing and planing conditions exist, the boat must be encouraged to plane as often and for as long as possible. Being able to work the waves is of particular importance. To catch the waves pump the spinnaker guy and sheet. The pump or pumps should be large yet smooth and in time with the helmsman pumping the mainsail. Good co-ordination between the crew and the helmsman is vital, not only in pumping the sails, but also using the crew movement to help steer the boat and help reduce drag-causing rudder movements. When the boat is sliding down the wave face the crew must heel the boat to

windward slightly, causing it to hang on to the wave for as long as possible. The action is similar to that of a surfer on a surf board.

Here is a summary of the sequence:

1    Wave under the bow  -  Crew slides forward.
     Spinnaker guy and sheet pumped.

2    Boat accelerates  -  Crew slides back.
     Boat is heeled to windward.

3    Boat slows  -  Boat heeled to leeward slightly.

4    Crew slides forward.

# 11 GYBING

The number and frequency of gybes varies from race to race. Big championship courses may call for only a few gybes, while small club racing courses often contain half a dozen or more. Whatever the number, good gybing technique will guarantee a gain over a competitor whose technique is less tidy. As in all boat handling techniques, the secret is to establish a firm sequence and routine.

## GYBING A SPINNAKER FROM RUN TO RUN

The easiest and most common type of gybe is from broad reach to broad reach or from run to run. During both, the spinnaker must be kept setting throughout as a collapsed sail will instantly reduce the boat's speed.

The responsibility for keeping the sail set rests with the helmsman who should steer the boat standing up with the tiller between his knees and spinnaker sheet and guy in each hand. The direction of the boat is controlled by moving the knees and ducking low during the gybe, with the spinnaker kept flying correctly throughout. Meanwhile the sequence for you, the crew, should run something as follows.
Before the gybe make sure that the centreboard is not too far up (with the risk of capsizing to windward), or too far down (with the possibility of tripping and capsizing to leeward).

**The helmsman must keep the spinnaker drawing during the gybe while the crew pulls the main boom across and then quickly re-sets the pole on the other side.**

Cleat the spinnaker guy and, with your free hand, tension the current windward jib sheet and cleat it and let off the leeward sheet. This means the jib is now preset and will need little alteration after the gybe. The helmsman should now have stood up, picked up the spinnaker guy and be steering with the tiller between his knees. Hand the spinnaker sheet back to him and stand up. Tension the leeward twinning line and release the windward one. As the helmsman starts the gybe release the inboard end of the pole, duck down and pull the boom across with the kicking strap. This pulling of the boom across the boat is vital, especially in stronger winds as the helmsman cannot use the mainsheet to do it because the spinnaker sheet and guy are occupying both his hands! After the gybe is completed the released inboard end of the spinnaker pole should be immediately to hand. Clip in the new guy and release the old and clip the pole onto the mast. Take the new sheet from the helmsman and then the guy and sit down on the windward side.

# GYBING A SPINNAKER FROM REACH TO REACH

The procedure for a close reach to close reach gybe differs slightly from that required for gybing on a run. Only in light winds is it feasible to have the helmsman standing and steering and controlling the sheet and guy. Once the wind increases it is more important to have the helmsman sitting quickly and hiking on the new windward side to keep the boat flat and under control. This means that you as the crew are responsible for the sheet and the guy.

The procedure should be as follows.

**Before the gybe** Check the centreboard position and preset the jib. If you are trapezing ask the helmsman to do both of these jobs for you. As the boat begins to turn for the gybe quickly square the pole back with one hand and ease the sheet with

the other: this stops the sail blowing between the jib and the mainsail after the gybe. As the boat begins to gybe let go the sheet and guy.

**During the gybe** Release the old twinning line with the hand that was holding onto the guy and with your other pull the new twinning line down, then grab the kicking strap and pull the boom across. Get quickly to the new windward side.

**Once the gybe is completed** Remove the inboard pole end from the mast and clip in the new guy. Push the pole forwards, not sideways and clip onto the mast. Pick up the spinnaker sheet from the helmsman who should have sheeted in the sail once the pole was clipped to the mast. Get ready to hike or trapeze.

**Boats without spinnakers should be gybed as quickly as possible to minimise speed loss. Here the boat hardly falls off the plane.**

# GYBING WITHOUT A SPINNAKER

On boats without a spinnaker the whole gybing sequence is very much quicker and the crew's main responsibility is to change sides and balance the boat, to trim the jib, and finally to make sure the boom comes across when required. In light winds roll the boat during the manoeuvre. This has the same effect as a roll tack and will maintain boatspeed throughout the gybe. Make sure the centreboard setting is correct before beginning the gybe. If you have any doubt as to how much to have up or down remember the words of a famous coaching friend of mine. " How much? " he said grinning wolfishly. " Just about enough to stand on if you capsize! "

# GYBING IN STRONG WINDS

In strong winds a gybe that goes wrong normally ends up as a swimming lesson while the people that get it right sail quickly away chuckling. In any class if dinghy the key to successful strong wind gybes is for the boat to be travelling fast going into the manoeuvre. The faster the boat is travelling the less the loads on the sails and rig that can cause the capsize. In waves the gybe must coincide with the boat planing down the face, while in flat water the boat must be gybed whilst travelling as fast as possible. Your responsibility as crew, apart from balancing the boat and handling the spinnaker and jib, is to help the mainsail across when the helmsman shouts "Now!" and turns the boat. Hesitation at this critical point will mean that the boat slows, the loads on the rig build substantially, and the

possibility of a capsize increases. Use one or even both hands to grab the kicking strap to pull the boom across and leave jobs like switching the twinning lines and releasing the pole until after the boat is safely on the new gybe.

As a final point, note that it is your responsibility as much as that of the helmsman to check that the kicking strap tension is correct before gybing. Too much tension and the likelihood of the boom end hitting the water during the gybe is high. This will cause the boat to head up and almost certainly capsize! Too little tension will encourage a windward roll prior to and after the gybe. Too much roll results inevitably in a capsize to windward!

To sum up, try to establish a set routine for every wind strength and each type of gybe and then, as with all other boat handling exercises, practice until the reactions become automatic.

# 12 CAPSIZING

It seems natural to follow the chapter on gybing with one on capsizing! Capsizing, or more correctly, the ability to recover quickly from a capsize, is a skill which every top crew must acquire.

First, a capsize while racing does not mean the race is over for you.

Quite the contrary; if it is windy enough for you to capsize, it is probably windy enough for your opponents to do the same and many a race has been won on a crew's ability to recover quickly. Second, if you never capsize in practice the chances are you are not driving hard enough. A windy practice is an ideal time to discover just what you can and cannot do with yourself and your boat. So what if you do capsize in

practice! You can really only end up wet, but you may be sure that a valuable lesson has been stored away!

## A CAPSIZE WITH THE SPINNAKER

If the capsize is the result of a small error in lightish conditions, try righting the boat with the spinnaker still hoisted. If this is possible you will be able to sheet in and continue very quickly.

If the wind is strong the best course of action is to take the spinnaker down before righting, otherwise the flogging sail will probably capsize the boat again. Once either the helmsman or crew are standing

on the centreboard keeping the mast horizontal with the water, one person must swim to the inside of the boat, uncleat the spinnaker halyard, and pull the sail down. The boat can now be righted with less chance of an immediate re-capsize.

## SAN FRANCISCO ROLL

Righting the boat following a capsize which finished with the mast pointing upwind is always something of a problem because the moment the rig is lifted clear of the water, the tendency is for the boat to be blown over on top of you leaving you to make a second attempt to right it.

One way of dealing with this is for one member of the crew to hang on to the centreboard while the other hangs on to him. As the rig lifts from the water, you will be pushed beneath the surface and, providing you hold on, up the other side. Retaining your hold on the new weather side should prevent the boat from completing a second capsize to leeward. The sensation of being pushed under the water can be a little scary at first but, once mastered, the technique is very effective.

## THE FOREDECK TAP DANCE METHOD

Getting back into the boat can be hard work and often slow, so the foredeck tap dance method was designed to get one member of the crew into the boat as soon as it is upright.

**We've capsized with the spinnaker up. The crew prevents the boat from inverting while the helmsman swims round to the cockpit and lowers the spinnaker and takes down the pole. The helmsman then goes to the bow and swims it into the wind. The crew then brings the boat upright and takes control until the helmsman has clambered aboard once more.**

That person can then help the other in and prevent the boat from blowing over again to leeward.

One person stands on the centreboard as normal, the other swims to the bow and holds onto the jib luff or forestay at approximately chest level. He places one foot each side of the jib tack fitting and then the boat is brought upright by the person on the centreboard. The crew member at the bow remains hanging on and is quickly pulled up out of the water. Once the boat is upright he then walks along the foredeck into the boat.

One word of warning, however: this method should not be used if your boat has a thin, fragile foredeck!

## THE SCOOP METHOD

This is the procedure most commonly taught in sailing schools and basic sailing classes. It is however the slowest method and not usually used when racing, unless someone is tired or hurt.

One person stands on the centreboard, while the other swims the bow into the wind. When the boat is pointing roughly into the wind the person at the bow then swims round towards the middle of the boat and then floats horizontally beside the centreboard case. When the boat is brought upright there is now one person already in the boat ready to help the other aboard.

Finally, every attempt should be made to prevent the boat from turning turtle (mast pointing straight down). This normally happens when the helmsman or crew are too slow in either getting onto the centreboard or jumping into the water as the boat capsizes. Never remain sitting or hanging on to the gunwale for more than a few seconds or your weight will quickly invert the boat and make righting it harder and slower.

# PART THREE

# RACE

# RESPONSIBILITIES

# 13 CREWING IN A RACE

So far we've looked at the mechanical actions that go to make a successful crew. This section covers the crew's racing responsibilities.

## BEFORE LEAVING THE SHORE

There are several things that must be attended to before you go afloat in order to make sure the forthcoming race is a success.

**Rig and check the boat** Rig the boat carefully, keeping your eyes open for any problems that have been missed when you last de-rigged the boat. If you have started rigging early enough you will have time to correct any problems that you come across, without feeling stressed and pressed for time.

**Food and drink for the day** If you are going to be out on the water all day, as you often are in a championship or open meeting, you must take sufficient food and drink.

On the day of the race, check the boat over carefully. Keep yours eyes open for potential problems.

The problem is that sufficient food and drink will be a significant weight, and this extra weight is undesirable and must be stowed where the weight will have minimum adverse effect. Personally I always try to tape the drink and lunch as near as possible to the pitch centre. In most boats this is towards the rear end of the centreboard case. If in doubt, always take more fluid than you think you will need, especially in hot weather when dehydration can be a real problem. Any drink that is not required can be poured overboard later.

**Find and make a note of the weather forecast** It is important that you are aware of any likely changes in wind strength and direction and if possible when the change will happen. Both will have a direct effect on your strategy during the race and, to a lesser degree, influence the clothing and other gear you need to take afloat.

**The sailing instructions and course** For a championship you should have read the sailing instructions the evening before the first race, but for an open meeting they will be given to you when you enter. Take a 10 minute coffee break after rigging the boat and before getting changed and read the instructions thoroughly, noting any unusual or important points. Always take them afloat, preferably in a plastic bag to keep them dry and readable.

**Select your clothing for the day** What to wear? Too much clothing and you risk becoming overheated and uncomfortable, too little and the day can be miserably cold. I always dress to feel comfortable and not too hot, my reasoning is that during the race, pumping adrenalin and the high work load will keep me warm. After the race has finished, and especially while waiting in between races, I make sure there is a another light jacket stowed dry to slip on to maintain correct body temperature. If you have a coach boat or a rescue boat available, always make use of this to dump gear and drink.

If the class of boat you sail allows you a weight jacket, always leave the shore with it full. If the conditions do not warrant wearing it, either dump the water over the side before the start or give the jacket to a coach or rescue boat. The real headache is when the forecast is for strong winds, but at start time the conditions are light. Then you have to assess the chances of the breeze increasing during the race. If this seems likely, I normally keep the weight jacket full and sling it over the centreboard case to minimise the damage the extra weight is doing. When the breeze increases the jacket can be put on. If the wind does not materialize at about half way round the course, then pour the water over the side.

Your clothing should be light and cool in light and medium conditions. Increase the layers as the breeze comes up. Your footwear, especially in trapeze boats, must provide good grip and enable you to move nimbly around the boat, so avoid heavy , hard soled-boots and choose instead lightweight, foot-hugging boots with a thin sole.

Make sure your harness or hiking pants are comfortable and that the buoyancy aid that you choose is close fitting and allows good freedom of movement. Gloves will probably be required, especially if the boat has been properly prepared with the minimum diameter sheets.

**Before you launch** Run through a mental check list including all of the above and these extra points:

▲ Do you have to sign on or take a tally with you?
▲ Have you all the weather / tidal information you need?
▲ Are the correct sails on board?
▲ Is the boat and its equipment legal? (Do you have to carry anchors, paddles, tow rope, etc?)
▲ Have you been to the toilet?

# RESPONSIBILITIES PRE - START

Once you arrive at the start area, set the boat correctly for the conditions of the day and head off upwind for a few minutes on each tack. This period before the start is important for understanding what the wind is doing and determining your plan for the start, the first beat and maybe subsequent beats.

Remember - upwind, the crew is the tactician. Sailing upwind on both tacks prior to the start gives you an opportunity to establish the relevant compass headings (see next chapter), and checking which side of the beat is favoured (read the Fernhurst book - *Tactics* by Rodney Pattisson).

**Once you arrive in the starting area use the remaining time constructively. Sail upwind to check rig settings and check for windshifts.**

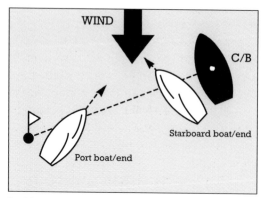

In this example, a boat from the starboard end crosses the line at a better angle than a boat on port near the other end, so the starboard end is favoured.

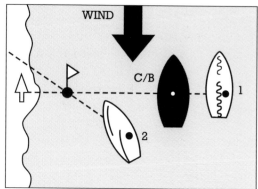

Get a line sight (or transit) by lining up both ends with an object (fixed!) on the shore.

Always jot the compass headings down with a chinagraph in an obvious place.

Make sure you are back in the start area a few minutes before the race committee fires the warning signal as this will give you enough time to check the start line.

Determine which end of the start line is favoured by using either the compass (see section on compass work) or by observing

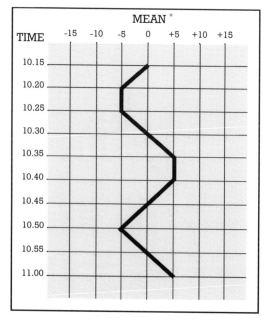

other boats coming off each end of the line. Remember that if the line is heavily biased towards one end, you might want to consider starting slightly away from the mass of boats that will congregate there to make sure of getting away in clearer air.

As the warning gun fires start your watch countdown. I always find it useful to set two watches. I wear one and put the other in the boat somewhere so that I have some back-up should one stop working.

Sail down to beyond one or both ends of the start line and try to obtain a transit; this is the key to knowing exactly where you are on the line and becomes vital should a disqualification rule come into force (such as after a general recall). By sighting down the line, lining up both ends and a fixed object on the shore you can now approach the line and know exactly how far back from it or over it you are. If possible try to get an accurate transit from both ends, that way if you are covered by other boats you still have the transit to fall back upon.

In this example, tracking the wind every five minutes shows that the shifts are fairly rythmic, back and forth.

If the committee boat displays the windward mark compass heading write it down, then work out the reach and run leg headings (see the later section on compasses). Jot these down too, preferably somewhere where they are easily seen.

At or just after the preparatory signal, raise the centreboard to check that it is clear of weed and make sure the boat is dry and the sheets tidy. Discuss quickly the planned starting place and the strategy for the first beat. At this stage it is often worth standing up briefly in the boat and looking upwind to observe any gusts or lulls that will arrive at or shortly after the start. Again these might influence which way you elect to go.

While the helmsman is positioning the boat in the required place you must make sure that the settings are correct for the conditions at the start. Check that the jibsheet leads, cunningham, outhaul and kicker tension, etc, are all set for the present windstrength. Call out the time remaining clearly, at 10 second intervals and then each second for the final half minute.

In the final few seconds before the start you as the crew must keep the helmsman informed of the situation around the boat. The helmsman can easily see boats just to windward, but there is a blind spot immediately behind and to a lesser degree to leeward of the jib. Boats coming in from this area must be pointed out before they have a chance to steal into the gap you have created to leeward. If you spot them early enough the helmsman will discourage them by bearing away and then quickly luffing back up, thereby putting them to

windward of you or forcing them to continue down the line.

Keep an eye on boats to leeward and ahead or hidden behind the jib. Keep the helmsman informed as to their movements, whether they are luffing, slowing, bearing away, etc, so that the helmsman is always able to position your boat to best advantage.

As you accelerate away from the line keep the helmsman informed all the time on the position of boats close to you. The information should be something like:

"We've got the boat immediately to leeward pointing slightly higher, we won't roll him before he gets to us." On hearing this information the helmsman will point the boat slightly higher.

Or "The boat to windward is lower and faster. At this angle he will roll us first." This information tells the helmsman that the boat must be sailed slightly freer and faster.

Remember, off the start line you control how fast or slow, how high or low the boat is sailing.

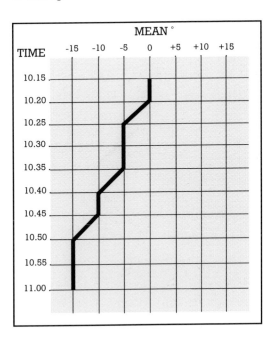

**In this example, the wind is progressively backing/shifting left, indicating a permanent shift.**

# UPWIND RESPONSIBILITIES

Because the crew does not have to concentrate on steering the boat and has a good all round view from his position in the boat he is able to call or contribute to the upwind tactics. Some helmsman like to have all but the very close boat-to-boat tactics called for them, others prefer to have the crew relay information on wind, other boats, etc, and then make the calls themselves. Whatever the arrangement on your boat, you should have a good understanding of basic upwind tactics.

The compass headings that you recorded before the start are now your reference to determine whether you are being headed or lifted. The basic rule is 'Try to sail on the lifted tack' as this should mean you are taking the shortest course to the windward mark. However there are other factors that may influence your decision on which way to go:

**Your overall tactical plan** Is one side of the beat favoured more heavily than the other? If so your plan should be to sail to that side. Occasionally that might mean sailing on headers to get there.

**Fleet awareness** Keep an eye on what the majority of the fleet are doing. Be aware of your position relative to the largest mass of boats and plan your tactics accordingly. The easiest way to visualize your position relative to the fleet is to imagine you are viewing the race from above, perhaps from a balloon or helicopter. It is much easier to work out the gains and losses in shifty conditions when imagining the race from a plan view.

While it is important that you sail your own race, bear in mind that occasionally you will be wrong so keep an eye on the

others. If the whole fleet heads left and you charge off to the right the chances are that they know something you don't. The key to successful fleet sailing is to stay in touch and not go out on a limb!

**Risk aversion** Sailors who take tactical risks rarely win an important series or championship.

The larger the number of races that go towards the result, the more conservative you need to be with your tactics. Taking flyers towards one corner or another in an attempt to win the race will occasionally give you a first, but more often than not it will drop you well down the fleet. As an example, at the 1988 Olympic trials we sailed a ten race series held in a variety of conditions over nearly two weeks. We won the event and subsequent Olympic selection, but did not win a single race. Instead we finished every race bar one (discarded) inside the top six, while some of our competitors won two or three races but then had to count results in the teens and twenties!

**Boat to boat tactics** As the race progresses the tactical considerations change subtly, the boat-to-boat tactics becoming more important.
For example, in a fleet of say 80 boats, tactically it's crucial to get the first beat right. All 80 boats will be very close together, so gains or losses can be very large indeed. As the race progresses the distance between the first and last boat grows, and therefore the potential for large gains or losses decreases. Instead, while you need to watch the fleet behind, the tactical importance shifts to small groups or individual boats. Your losses and gains will be made there.

Like chess, sailing tactics follow a set pattern of guidelines. For nearly every occasion when one boat meets another there is a move and also a counter move. Unfortunately, in this book we have not the space to include boat-to-boat tactics along with overall strategy in any sort of detail. There are two ways to learn: first by sailing and learning by your mistakes and second by reading and learning from suitable books. A combination of both is ideal!

## OTHER UPWIND RESPONSIBILITIES

Of course you have other things to think about when going upwind. Boat balance and trim have to be continually altered according to wind strength and sea state. The jib settings and leads must always be correct to keep the boat at maximum speed, while the jibsheet is continually adjusted in gusty winds or choppy water. The helmsman needs to know about approaching waves that could slow the boat as well as any obstructions such as weed, flotsam, fishing boats, cruisers etc that could get in the way. Keep an eye on approaching clouds or weather fronts, gusts or lulls, tide lines or decreasing or increasing tidal flow. In fact you need to observe anything and everything that could affect the outcome of the race.

## KEEPING MORALE AND CONFIDENCE HIGH

Nothing slows a boat more quickly than one or other of the crew getting angry or depressed about the race. In every race mistakes will be made and moods will fluctuate. The winners, however, try to make fewer mistakes, but also accept them when they do happen and don't dwell on

them or become upset. This is part of a correct winning attitude and like everything else, has to be worked on and practised until it's automatic.

Each person in the boat is therefore responsible for lifting the other when anger or depression is apparent. Positive comments help to lift flagging spirits, for example: " Hey, we all make mistakes, lets forget it and get back in touch " or " Forget it, we've got great speed today, let's pass these guys and win the race. "

Sometimes a well-timed joke can instantly put the situation into perspective and lighten the atmosphere. Whatever happens, during the race is not the time to discuss the problem, criticise or say " I told you so." Wait until you get ashore to discuss openly what went wrong and how to avoid making the same mistake again. Our 470 coach Rob Andrews summed it all up:

" If you want to win, act professionally. "

## DOWNWIND RESPONSIBILITIES

Once the windward mark is rounded the tactical responsibilities shift from the crew to the helmsman. Now, you as the crew have to concentrate on making the boat go as fast as possible.

However, you are still responsible for three other duties:

### CALL THE LIFTS AND THE HEADERS WHEN SAILING ON A RUN

Because you are sailing downwind, the windshifts that you experienced going upwind do not simply disappear and the luff and angle of the spinnaker is just as accurate in picking them up as any jib luff or indication from the compass. When running downwind the wind heads when, without any change in course, the pole needs to be eased forward to set the sail correctly. A lift is indicated by the pole having to be brought aft. Your calls determine the optimum angle the boat can be sailed downwind. A header means the boat can be borne away and hopefully sailed closer to the direction of the next mark. A lift means the boat has to be sailed higher.

## CHECK THE HELMSMAN'S BLIND SPOTS

If the helmsman is sitting on the leeward side there is a large area from underneath the boom, to just past the jib tack, where boats and obstructions are very hard to see. You must inform the helmsman of any problems in these areas so action can be taken to avoid them.

**When sailing downwind the crew should call the lifts and headers.**

This is particulary relevant after just rounding the windward mark in a large fleet as there (hopefully!) will be many boats still heading upwind, behind you, and some of them will be in that blind spot.

If the helmsman is sitting on the windward side, such as in a non-spinnaker boat, the blind spot is the same as for going upwind, namely behind the jib.

## CALLING THE' PRESSURE' IN THE SAIL

In light winds not only must you call the lifts and headers, but also the angle at which the spinnaker is working best. The boat cannot be sailed dead downwind in these conditions and instead must be sailed more on a broad reach to raise the apparent wind speed and so increase boatspeed. Sail too low and the wind pressure in the spinnaker will become too light. Sail too high and the pressure in the sail will be good, but the heading towards the mark will be poor. Optimum progress towards the next mark is achieved by a combination of good pressure, while sailing as low as possible. To help establish this, good communication between crew and helmsman is essential and a running commentary needs to be maintained by you.

For example:

Crew: " There's a little gust. I've good pressure now "

Helmsman: " Ok, bearing away slightly on that "

Crew: " That's good there. No lower or I'll be too light "

Crew: " Ok, I'm a little light now "

Helmsman: " Heading up slightly, then "

And so on. This kind of communication leads to the boat sailing the optimum course downwind.

# COMPASS WORK

In the past compasses were found only on the top flight racing dinghies, and even at that level were often only for show. Now they are standard equipment on most boats and it is important that you know how to use them.

The range and complexity of compasses varies, but I believe that the large simple ones are the best. Large so that they can be seen clearly by both helmsman and crew even in the roughest conditions and simple so that it is easy to remember courses and bearings.

The compass must be mounted in a position that:
▲ Both helmsman and crew can see clearly.
▲ Is approximately in normal line of sight.

Both of these requirements mean that the compass has to be positioned in one of the following places: 1. In the side tanks or foredeck forward of the crew. 2. Hung just beneath the gooseneck on the mast, or 3. Flush at mast gate level. Compasses that are mounted either on the back of the centreboard case, or worse, low in the cockpit floor are out of the line of sight and therefore awkward and distracting to use.

Once mounted in the right place, a compass should be used for the following:
▲ Identifying windshifts.
▲ Checking the starting line.
▲ Establishing the gybe and leeward mark angles.
▲ Windshift tracking before the start.

The first and most common use of a compass is to identify whether you are being lifted or headed when sailing upwind. For example, you are sailing on starboard tack with the compass giving a reading of 220 degrees. A few minutes later a small gust appears and the compass now reads 210 degrees. This tells you that the wind has shifted 10 degrees to the left and, on this course, you have been headed. If the

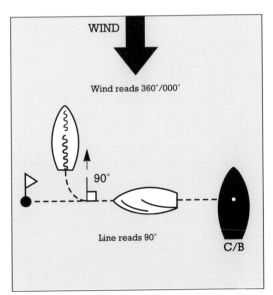

In this example, the line is at a 90 degree angle to the wind and no end is favoured.

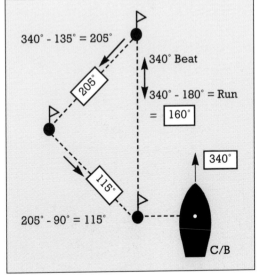

Windward mark bears 340 degrees. Run - 160 degrees. 1st reach - 205 degrees. 2nd reach - 115 degrees.

heading had swung to 230 degrees, you would have been given a lift of 10 degrees. You of course then have to decide whether to tack or stay on the present tack.

As you approach a windward mark, remember the port and starboard headings you had near the leeward or start mark. When you eventually turn the leeward mark to go back upwind again, recall those numbers and check them with your current heading, this way you know instantly whether you are on the lifting or heading tack.

The compass can also be used to determine accurately which end of the starting line is favoured.

Sail down to one end of the starting line. Line up both ends and note the compass bearing, then sail to approximately the middle of the line and take a head-to-wind reading, ie note the compass bearing when

the boat is pointing exactly into the eye of the wind. In the example shown, the line reading is 090 degrees and the wind is 360 degrees, this means that the line is square, with neither favoured. If, however, the wind reading was 350 degrees, this would mean that the port end was favoured by 10 degrees.

In the example I've used nice round numbers for illustration, if however your mental arithmetic is as bad as mine and the numbers awkward, use a chinagraph pencil on the side tanks to avoid any errors.

In championships and large open meetings or regattas it is usual for the race committee to display the compass bearing to the first windward mark. From this bearing you can work out the reciprocal or reverse bearing which gives you the leeward mark bearing from the windward mark. For example, the windward mark

The Silva compass is easy to read, but magnification is low.

The Plastimo compass magnifies and the reading is approximately the same on port and on starboard tacks, so it's easy to remember.

bears 340 degrees, and the bearing of the leeward mark from the weather mark is 340 - 180 = 160 degrees.

Provided the race committee has promulgated the bearing of the gybe mark from the weather mark, you will be able to calculate the course for both reaches.

In the example used, which represents a normal championship course, we know the committee will try for a 45 degree course and the windward mark is bearing 340 degrees. 340-135 degrees equals 205 degrees which is the first reach bearing, then 205-90 equals the second reach bearing, which here is 115 degrees. Note all of the bearings down in chinagraph ready for instant reference. The real advantage of this exercise arises when the course is big and the marks are small and difficult to see even in good visibility. With the bearings worked out you can sail on the compass until the marks become clear.

Windshift tracking can help your understanding of the day's wind and its behaviour. Either by using a prepared permanent tracking chart or simply jotting the port and starboard headings down one under the other every two, four or five minutes, you will soon see if there is a pattern or trend in the shifts.

**Particularly when beating, always remain alert for possible windshifts.**

# 14 AFTER THE RACE

Bang! The finishing gun goes, hopefully signifying that you have finished high up and in the chocolates. Time now to relax and contemplate on the race and any mistakes made.

If the race has gone badly the chances are the atmosphere in the boat will be slightly strained. The normal sign is a sullen silence between helmsman and crew, probably each blaming the other for a poor result. This is not a good environment in which to discuss the race, as each person will be very defensive and resentful of criticism. Instead restore the communication between helmsman and crew and find the bright side. One or other of you, and it is usually the crew(!), must break the silence and start putting the race into perspective. Look around and see who else has had a bad day (you're never alone!), crack a joke, or laugh at a situation that seemed bad during the race. In short, try to raise the spirits of both yourself and your partner.

As mentioned before, personal criticism is always hard to swallow, so when individual mistakes crop up, always handle the situation with tact and diplomacy. Once the atmosphere is lightened, mistakes and errors that were made can be discussed openly and corrected for the future.

An example:
Imagine a tight port and starboard situation where you had been sailing the boat on port tack. You called "Not crossing" but your helmsman said "Yes we are". In the end you didn't make it and a collision occurred.

Now it's tempting to whisper something like "Why the hell don't you listen to me?" and appear wonderfully righteous. Instead you must share the responsibility and say something like "In those crossing situations we must play it safe, I'll try to tell you earlier about starboard tackers in future so we have more time to decide what action to take." From what you have said the helmsman can recognise the mistake was his, yet because you have shared the responsibility, and said 'we', the criticism does not appear personal.

The best time to discuss a race is on the way back to the shore, as once on terra firma you will find that you will be too busy to give the matter the attention it deserves.

## BOAT MAINTENANCE

Having come ashore after a hard race it is always tempting to postpone any jobs that need doing until before the race following morning, especially when you're tired, wet and hungry. But as we all know, jobs always seems to take twice as long as expected so the evening after the race is always the best time to start.

## PERSONAL MAINTENANCE

Let's look at four areas:

▲ Diet
▲ Sleep
▲ Drink
▲ Play !!

**Diet** Nowadays the importance of a correct and healthy diet is being stressed continually in everyday life, so we're nearly all aware of what we should be eating. The main area of misunderstanding is when to eat.

Sailing can be an athletic and demanding sport. During a windy race you use nearly as many calories as a middle distance runner, and it's vital that the energy reserves you have depleted during the day are topped up again. Like a battery, if you continuously use energy without re-charging, the amount of power and energy you produce will gradually dwindle. This is particularly relevant over a long regatta or championship, when five or six days of hard sailing can leave you tired and lethargic.

Unlike a rechargeable battery, the human body does not need to be connected up to the mains!

Instead, all we need do to re-charge is eat the right foods at the right time. The right time is as soon as possible after the race has finished, so the first action on arriving ashore after a windy race is to find some food and drink. Avoid chocolate, sweets, ice cream, etc, instead eat food high in carbohydrates such as potatoes, bread, pasta and bananas, as these are what your body needs to produce energy.

Avoid the usual trap of heading for the bar first and then remembering much later that you had better find a bite to eat, which usually turns out to be a burger or fish and chips. While the food itself is not energy producing, the lateness of the hour will prevent your body converting it into the energy you need ready for the next day.

**Get the support boat to pass you food and drink as soon as possible after the finish.**

Always eat early then, if needs be, drink later.

There are now several drinks available on the market which are very high in carbohydrates and are designed to be consumed immediately after exercise. The advantage of having your food in a liquid form is the ease with which it is prepared and then kept in a small, light drinks container. This is not a substitute for a proper evening meal, but it will contribute to the body's re-charge by providing

carbohydrates in a convenient, easy to consume form. Not as tasty as a sandwich perhaps, but certainly easier to take afloat and ready for use as you sail for the shore after the race!

At the time of writing, these energy drinks are relatively new to the world of sailing, but I am sure that more and more crews will make use of them.

**Sleep**  Different people need a different amount of sleep. Some can thrive on four hours, others need eight or ten. You will know how much you need, so it is important to keep to your routine during a sailing event.

Lack of sleep affects our mental health rather than our physical health and as sailing is very much a mental game, it is important that you are rested and sharp before each race. It is always tempting to stay up late drinking, partying, or just yarning at an event, but repeated late nights, unless you are used to them, will leave you tired and jaded the next morning. Try to stick to your usual number of hours of sleep.

**Drinks**  Both non-alcoholic and alcoholic drinks should be considered. The more important is obviously non-alcoholic as we must take in sufficient liquid daily just to survive. Dinghy sailors are very prone to dehydration, even during winter races. The exercise we do and the clothes we wear contribute directly to a dehydrated state. Dry suits, wet suits, waterproofs are all designed to keep us warm or dry, but the drawback can be a high level of sweating and subsequent danger of dehydration. As an example - a recent sailing event saw me struggling to get below an imposed maximum weight limit. I put on some thermal wear and over the top my dry suit

and set off for a half hour run. I came back and weighed myself again. The amount I lost was nearly one kilo. This was just water loss and was indicative of how much we probably lose over the course of an average race. If we allow our bodies to become too dehydrated the outcome is the same as not eating properly - tiredness, slow reactions and lethargy.

So not only should water or some soft drink be taken afloat, but also consumed in quantity ashore if we are to remain on peak form for the next day's sailing.

Do not forget that alcohol has a severely dehydrating effect upon the body which may prove to be detrimental to both concerntration and stamina during a race following a heavy night in the bar. Drinking water after taking onboard certain spirits - even the evening before - may regenerate a feeling of intoxication; this is particularly true where aniseed-based drinks are concerned.

It is your decision as to the amount of alcoholic drink you have after a race. Over indulgence must be detrimental to your performance on the race course and this is unfair to your partner. Certainly sailing should be fun, and part of that fun is enjoying yourself at events, and you must decide just how seriously you are going to take each event. In the interests of maintaining a good relationship between you and your partner I recommend that you avoid going overboard in the bar, have one or two to relax, but know your limit.

**Play!**  We'll leave that to you....

Opposite: the author, in the Barcelona Olympics pulls the clew of the spinnaker round, ready for a gybe-set onto a run.

# PART 4

# MASTERCLASS

# 15 ASYMMETRIC SPINNAKERS & TWIN-WIRE BOATS

Like everything else in this world, sailing is subject to change and the technology does not stand still. It is human nature to continually try to improve, make lighter, stronger, go faster, etc, and racing sailboats is no different.

The demand for high performance, low maintenance, fun to sail dinghies continues to grow and new boats with larger and larger sail plans including asymmetrical spinnakers are appearing on the market. In order to accept all the extra power, boats are being designed with wings or racks that either just the crew, or both helmsman and crew can trapeze from. These boats present new challenges and difficulties for the modern crew.

Even if they have not sailed with one, most crews will know what an asymmetric spinnaker looks like. These sails are essentially large, very full genoas which replace the traditional spinnaker. Instead of a spinnaker pole, a single spar projecting from the bows of the boat is used to support the leading edge of the sail. The clew is controlled by two sheets (one either side) in a similar fashion to the jib and so the crew has only one sheet to worry about at a time, as opposed to a traditional spinnaker, which has a sheet and a guy.

The sail is trimmed in the same way as a conventional spinnaker, with the luff curling continually.

**The demand for high performance, low maintenance, fun-to-sail dinghies is increasing.**

Apart from the problems which their sheer size can introduce, the sails are easier to use and control than a symmetrical spinnaker..

The controls and fittings used on boats with asymmetric spinnakers differ from those on boats carrying a traditional spinnaker and within each class there are further differences, but there are three or four key controls which are common.

**The pole** The pole is normally housed inside the boat when not required, and 'launched' when the spinnaker is set. A pulley arrangement thrusts the pole outboard, and it is usually returned into the boat when the spinnaker is dropped with the assistance of a powerful shock-cord system. Poles are made from either glass fibre or aluminium alloy and are designed to have a certain amount of bend when in use. The newcomer may find this flexing rather alarming at first.

**The sheets** The sheets work very much like jib sheets except that the lazy sheet will be around the jib luff depending on which gybe you are on. Trimming the sail is simply a matter of playing the working sheet. To gybe the sail, the working sheet is let go and the lazy sheet pulled in to take the sail around the jib luff to set the sail upon the new side. Because the sails are normally very big - as much as three or four times the sail area of main and jib combined - ratchet blocks and gloves are usually needed to handle them in conjunction with sheets of generous diameter.

**Stowing** The sail is stowed either by hand in a bag, similar to a 470, Fireball, etc, (except that the bag is bigger and positioned in the middle of the boat) or it may be stowed in and launched from a chute.

**The chute** Makes for easy launching and recovery, but the bigger the sail the harder it is to pull in and the larger the chute needed. A bag is always used for large asymmetric spinnakers to avoid friction problems; bag stowage is also easier on the fabric of the sail. Of the two systems, the bag provides the crew with a little more work.

# SAIL HANDLING

There are obviously several differences in the way the asymmetric spinnaker is hoisted, trimmed and dropped compared to that of a symmetrical sail.

## HOISTING

Most of the classes using an asymmetric spinnaker have been designed along similar lines. They are nearly all aimed to be fast, exciting, and are mostly unstable. Although these factors encourage the boat to perform well, the drawback is that both helmsman and crew have to be very aware of their body weight positioning in the boat. Too much or too little weight on one side or other of the cockpit will result in an immediate swimming party, so hoisting the spinnaker requires good co-ordination between helmsman and crew.

Standard procedure is as follows: At the windward mark the boat is borne well away onto a broad reach, while the crew comes in off the trapeze, easing the jib and moving to balance the boat. Next, the pole is launched by the crew or perhaps the helmsman. The spinnaker is then hoisted (usually by the crew) and carefully sheeted in. The crew then balances the boat by progressively moving out, while the helmsman heads up to a closer course. Before the boat starts to heel, the crew clips on and goes out onto the trapeze taking the spinnaker sheet with him. In boats with twin trapezes the helmsman then clips on and starts to move out on the wire, taking tiller and mainsheet with him. This is the really hard bit for the helmsman in a twin-wire boat, so the crew must appreciate the difficulties and be ready to help matters either by moving inboard momentarily to balance the boat or easing the sheet if a capsize threatens or even simply grabbing the helmsman's collar and pulling him outboard!

## TRIMMING

Once up and drawing, the trimming of the sail is little different from that of a normal spinnaker, except that you have no spinnaker guy to worry about.

**The boats bears away and the pole is launched. Once hoisted, the spinnaker is trimmed and the crew clips on to the trapeze and moves outboard as the helmsman heads up. When the boat is settled, the helmsman begins trapezing, moving outboard steadily while sheeting in slightly on the main.**

The luff must be kept curling all the time, with the sheet being continually eased and trimmed. When a gust hits, the sheet is eased to compensate for the shift aft in apparent wind, and also because the helmsman will have borne away for maximum speed. As the boat accelerates the sheet will need to be trimmed in. If the breeze is very strong and the boat travelling near maximum speed, the helmsman will watch the luff of the spinnaker and steer accordingly, bearing away on a curl and luffing slightly when the luff flicks out. Concentration by both partners should be high, for a spinnaker that is allowed too much curl or even to collapse is almost certain to result in a sudden windward dunking or, possibly, a capsize to windward.

## GYBING

Gybing an asymmetric spinnaker is very easy compared to with a conventional sail. There is no pole to worry about changing over, twinning lines to release and pull or sheets to keep under control, instead the crew only has to worry about balancing the boat and pulling in the new sheet.

As the gybe mark is reached the crew or helmsman should uncleat the leeward jibsheet and cleat the windward. The jib is now preset for after the gybe. As the boat bears away for the gybe the crew moves inboard to balance the boat. The old spinnaker sheet is eased and the new one picked up in the other hand. As the mainsail crosses the boat the new sheet is pulled to bring the clew around the jib luff and onto the new side. The helmsman then brings the boat onto the new course, the crew clips onto the trapeze and balances the boat, while trimming the spinnaker.

The key to a successful gybe is keeping the boat travelling as fast as possible before and during the gybe. If the boat is allowed to slow down, the loads on the sails increase dramatically, making the boat unstable and prone to capsize.

## DROPPING

The fun eventually has to stop and the spinnaker has to be dropped and recovered. The boat must be borne away while the crew comes inboard. The crew then releases the spinnaker halyard and either pulls the sail into the chute or grabs

The secret to a successful gybe is to keep the boat moving fast throughout the manoeuvre.

the windward sheet and pulls the sail around the jib luff and then down into the bag.

About halfway through this operation a moment is taken to uncleat the pole launch system, letting the pole slide back into the boat. The spinnaker drop is finished and the sheets quickly tidied. The crew then hooks on to the trapeze and preparations are made to round the leeward mark in the usual manner.

During the drop, if the helmsman is also trapezing, it is normal for him to stay out on the wire throughout the evolution, compensating for the sudden decrease in power during the spinnaker drop by heading up slightly and heaving in on the mainsheet.

# TWIN-WIRING

An increasing number of classes permit both helmsman and crew to trapeze at the same time - obviously the helmsmen don't want the crews to have all the fun! This changes the crew's responsibilities.

## BOAT BALANCE

The helmsman's movements are restricted when steering from the trapeze so the crew is even more responsible for balance. Sailing upwind and down in gusty conditions sees the crew continually moving in and out, while the helmsman is able to do little more than bend or straighten his legs. In big gusts and lulls the crew may be trapezing flat out one moment and sitting down to leeward the next.

Because the helmsman is usually last out and last in, twin wire boats seem to favour a smaller, agile crew, combined with a larger, heavier helmsman: something to consider should you be looking at crewing a double trapeze boat.

## SAIL HANDLING

In conventional dinghies the helmsman hoists the spinnaker. In twin wire boats the crew is responsible for hoisting as well as dropping the sail, so the timing of mark roundings is altered slightly to allow for the extra job.

The mainsail and jib controls, such as kicker, cunningham, jib tack etc all need to be led to positions that both helmsman and crew can reach while trapezing. This is vital for key controls such as the kicker for example. In a lull the crew will be moving in to balance the boat and is therefore the best person to alter the kicker at the same time.

## COMMUNICATION

With the helmsman trapezing alongside you, communication is easy enough and there is no need to shout. The role the crew plays is still the same: as with conventional dinghies, twin wire boats still require maximum helm concentration going upwind, so the crew should still be responsible for the majority of tactics other than the close boat-to-boat calls. The helmsman out on the wire has a good all round view and full appreciation of the boats in the vicinity, so tactical calls can become more of a team effort. Remember - two sets of brains are better than one!

# Also published by Fernhurst Books

The Catamaran Book *by Brian Phipps*

Catamaran Racing *by Kim Furniss and Sarah Powell*

Championship Laser Racing *by Glenn Bourke*

First Aid Afloat *by Dr Robert Haworth*

The International Fourteen *by T.J. Vaughan*

Knots and Splices *by Jeff Toghill*

The Laser Book *by Tim Davison*

Laser Racing *by Ed Baird*

Mental & Physical Fitness for Sailing *by Alan Beggs & John Derbyshire*

Mirror Racing *by Guy Wilkins*

Racing: A Beginner's Manual *by John Caig & Tim Davison*

Racing Crew *by Malcolm McKeag*

Racing Skipper *by Robin Aisher*

The Rules in Practice 1993-96 *by Bryan Willis*

Sailing: A Beginner's Manual *by John Driscoll*

Sailing for Kids *by Gary & Steve Kibble*

Sailing the Mirror *by Roy Partridge*

Sailpower *by Lawrie Smith and Andrew Preece*

Sails *by John Heyes*

Tactics *by Rodney Pattisson*

Tides and Currents  *by David Arnold*

Topper Sailing *by John Caig*

Tuning Yachts and Small Keelboats *by Lawrie Smith*

Tuning Your Dinghy *by Lawrie Smith*

Weather at Sea *by David Houghton*

Wind Strategy *by David Houghton*

Helming to Win *by Ian Pinnell and Lawrie Smith*

Fernhurst Books are available from all good bookshops and chandleries.  In case of difficulty, or if you would like a copy of our full catalogue, please send your name and address to:

**Fernhurst Books, Duke's Path, High Street, Arundel, West Sussex  BN18 9AJ**